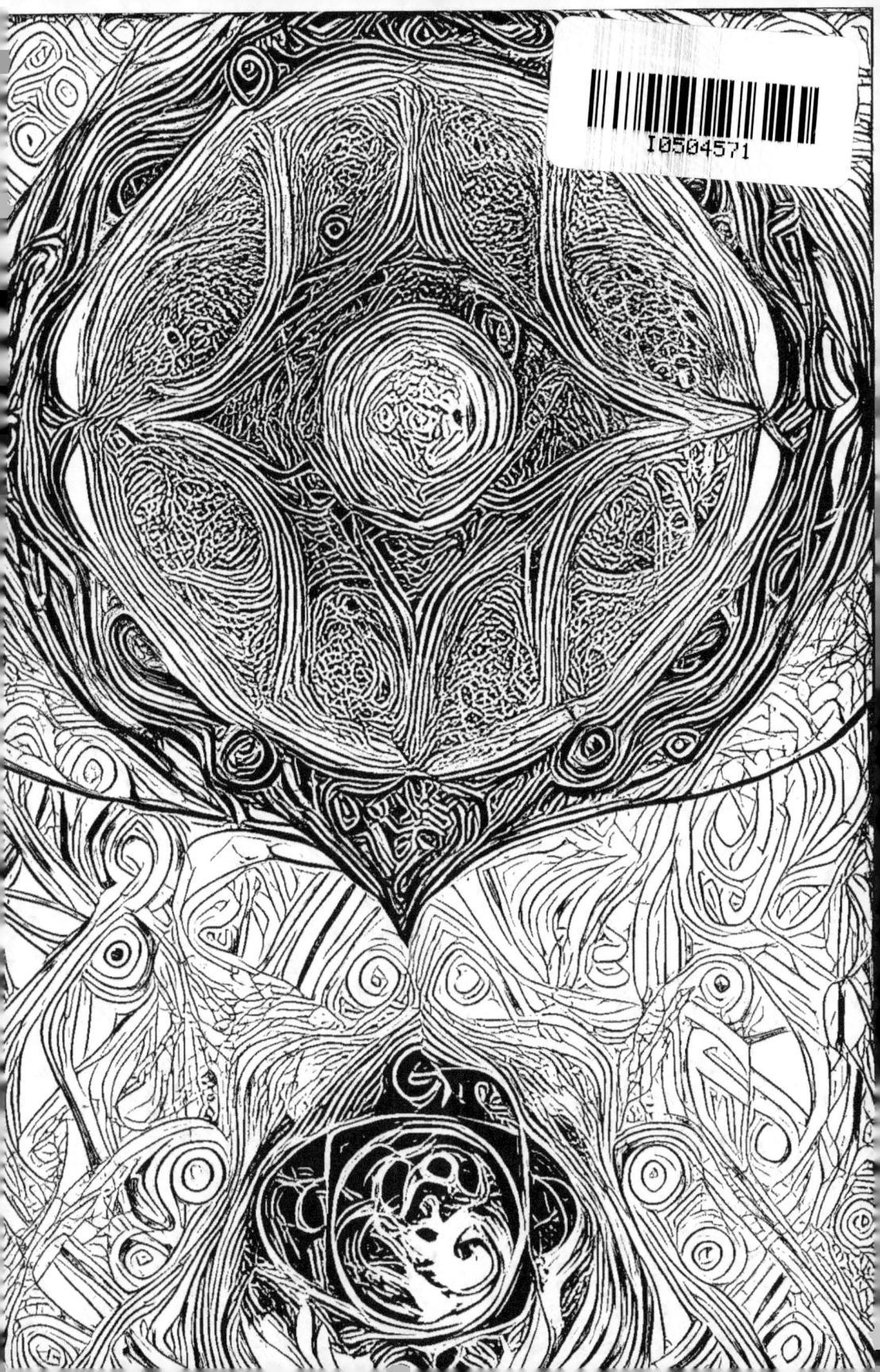

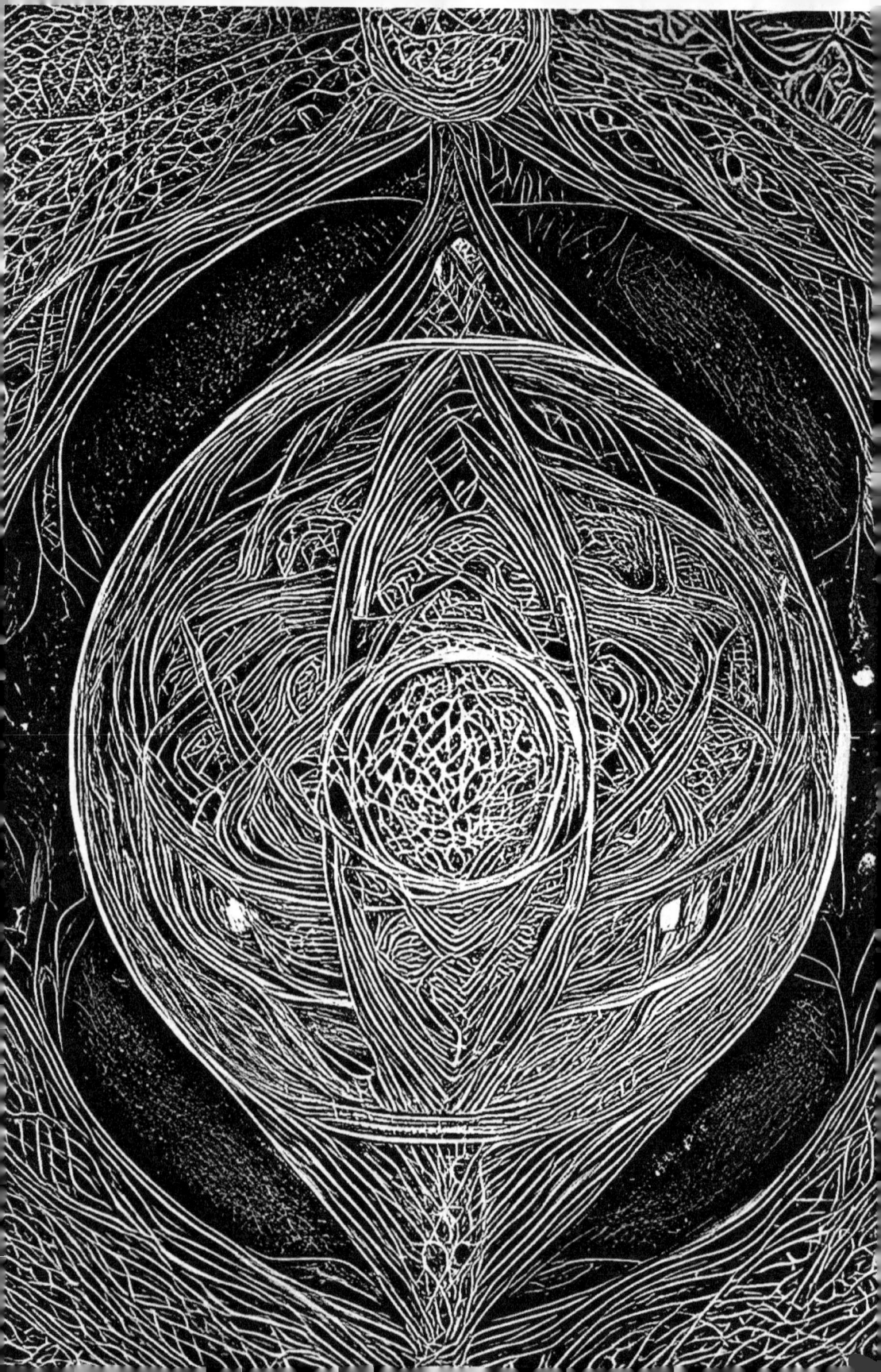

AI WICCAN COLORING BOOK

Hey there, I'm Jeremy Hubert Burt. I was feeling inspired and decided to use a prompt to create some 3D coloring book pages. The prompt I used was:

"Design a mesmerizing coloring book page featuring a captivating Wiccan symbol. Against a pristine white background, use bold black lines to illustrate the intricate details of the symbol, evoking a sense of magic and fascination.

Create ornate and enchanting background designs that complement the Wiccan symbol, immersing the viewer in a world of mysticism and wonder. These designs should inspire curiosity and a connection to nature.

Incorporate various shapes such as delicate curves, intertwined vines, and symbolic elements throughout the page, inviting individuals to explore the depths of Wiccan spirituality. Add captivating phrases in a font that captures the essence of nature and spirituality, enhancing the sense of enchantment and discovery.

Outline the symbol with bold black lines, clearly defining the boundaries for coloring. This empowers enthusiasts to infuse the symbol with their own interpretations and artistic expression, using the striking contrast of black and white.

The coloring book page promises a captivating journey into the realm of Wiccan symbolism. It invites individuals to delve into the art of coloring, providing a delightful sense of relaxation and stress relief. Embrace the magical power of the Wiccan symbol amidst the timeless contrast of black and white."

After creating the design, I decided to edit the levels in GIMP in greyscale image mode to give it that extra touch of depth and detail. The whole process only took me a day, and I'm really happy with the results. I even published the pages using the Sqribble ebook maker, which was super easy to use. Check out the link if you want to Publish Your eBook: https://bit.ly/3nVzjvK.

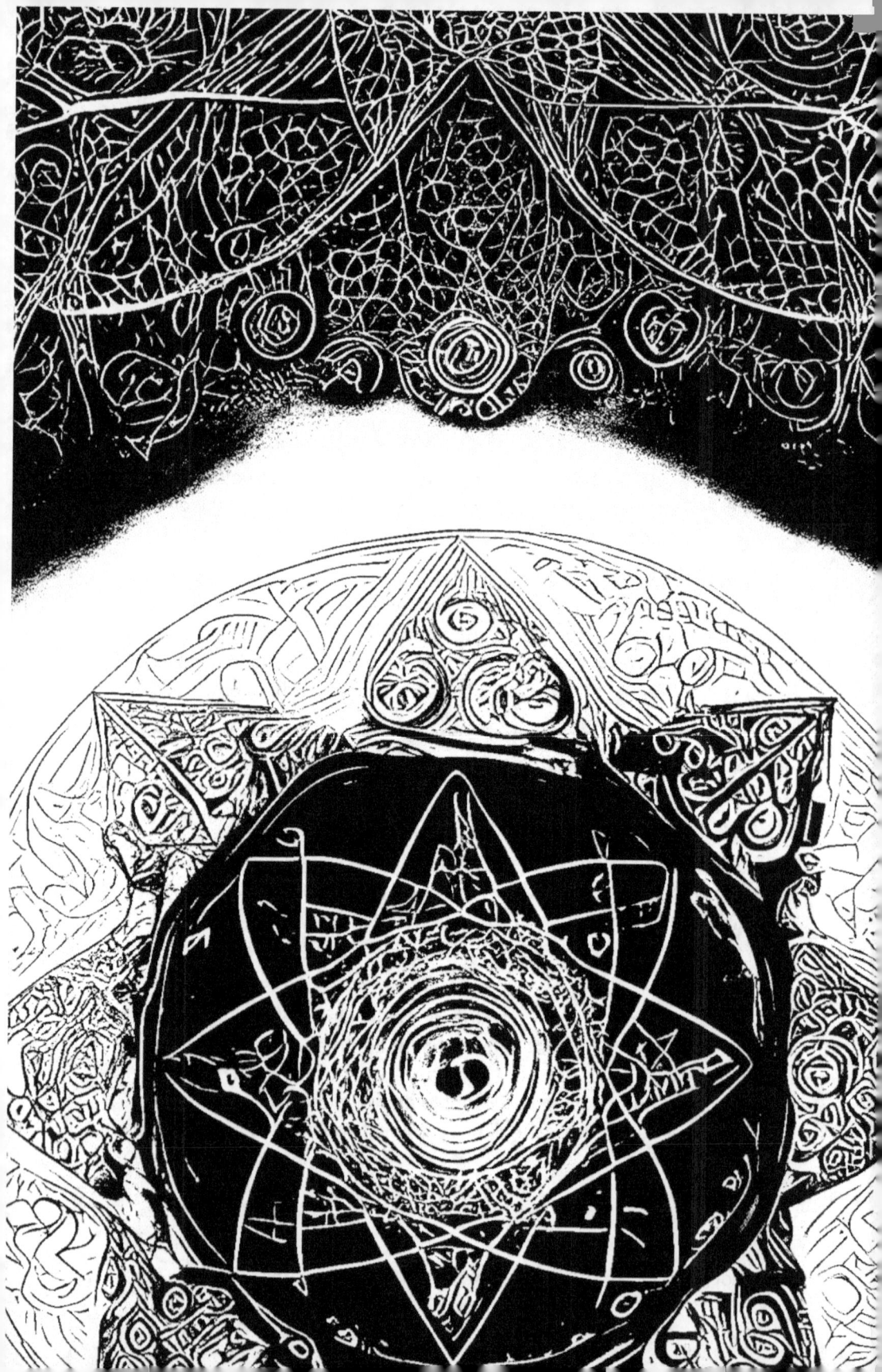

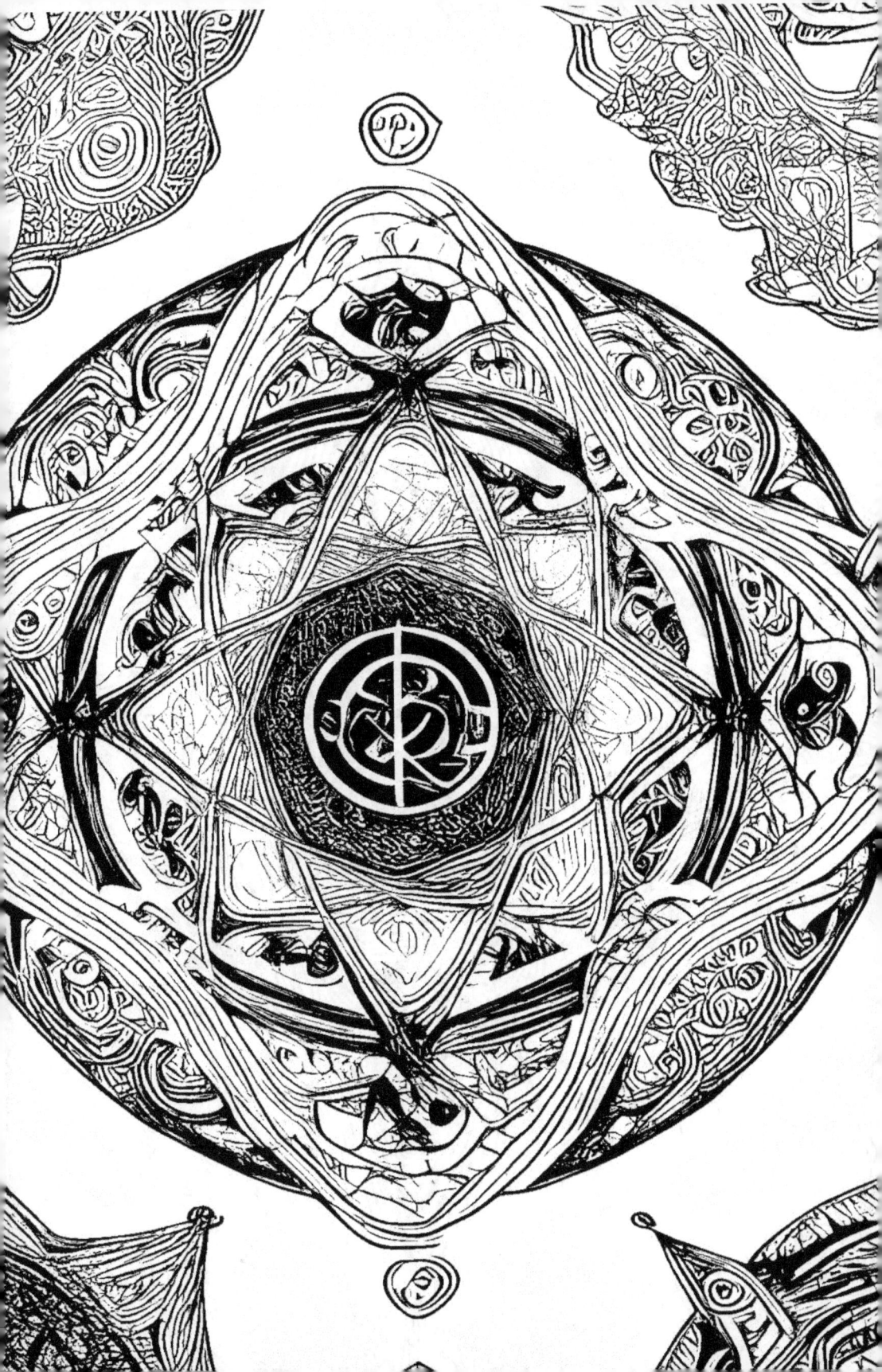

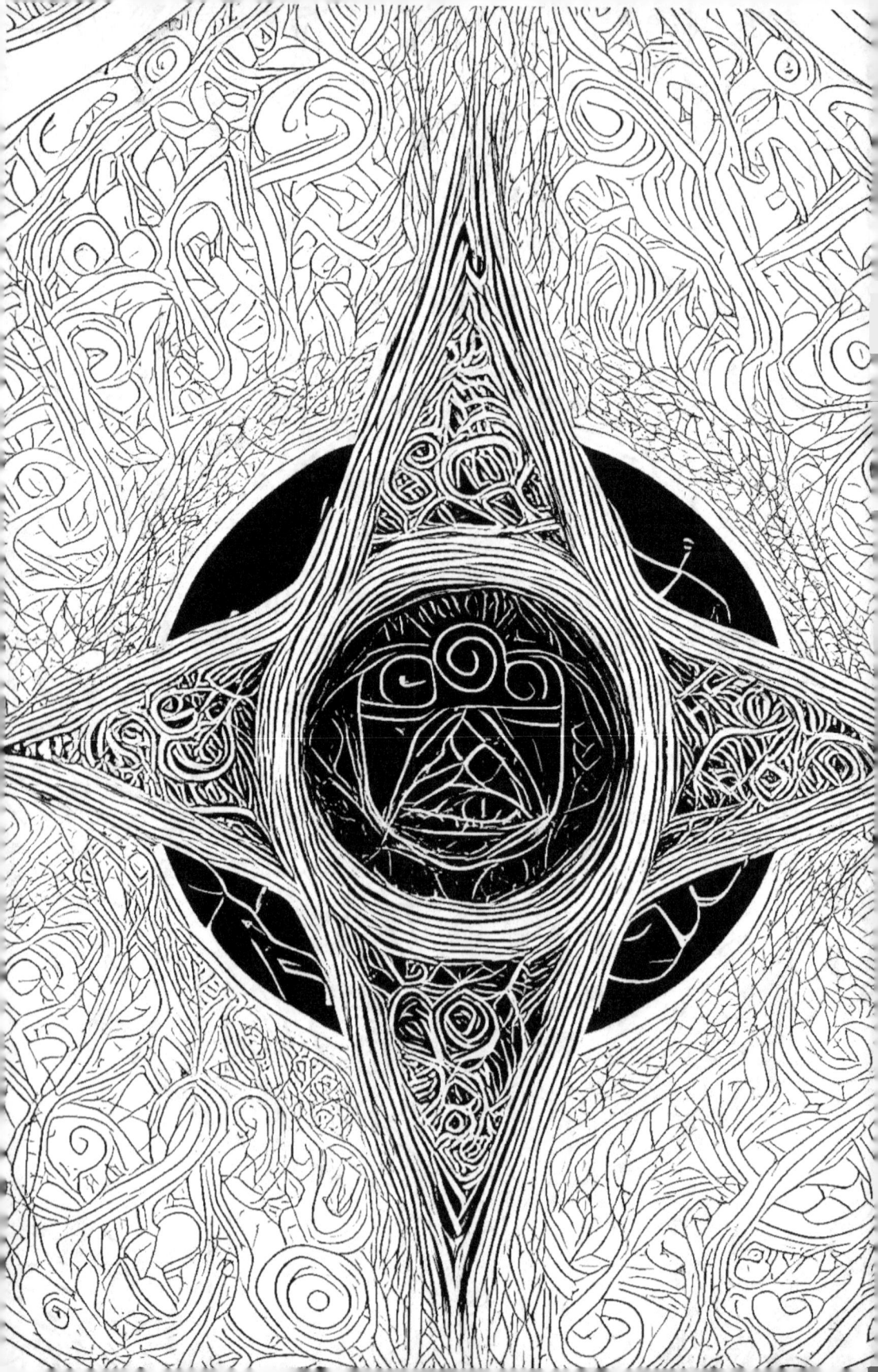

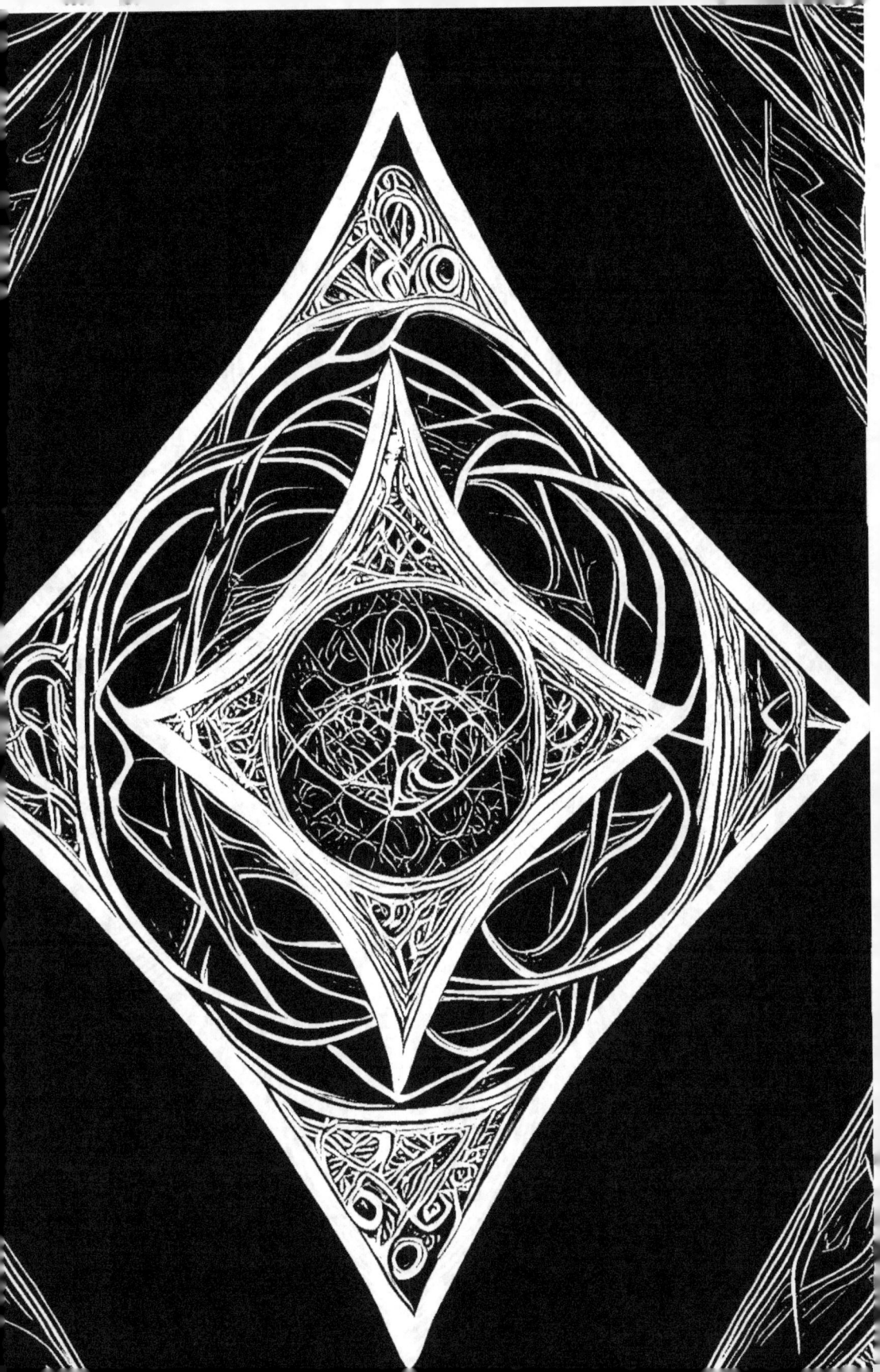

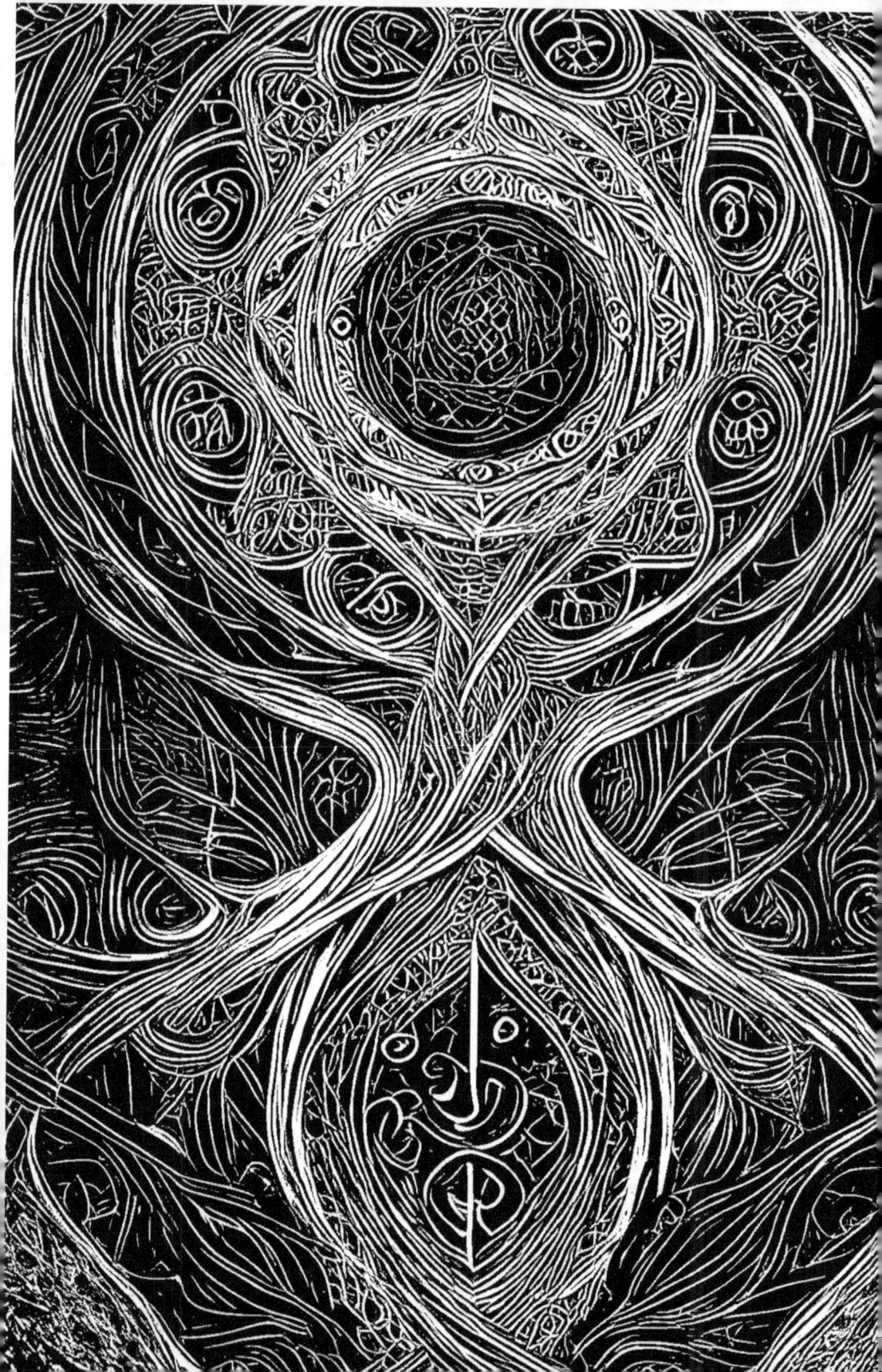

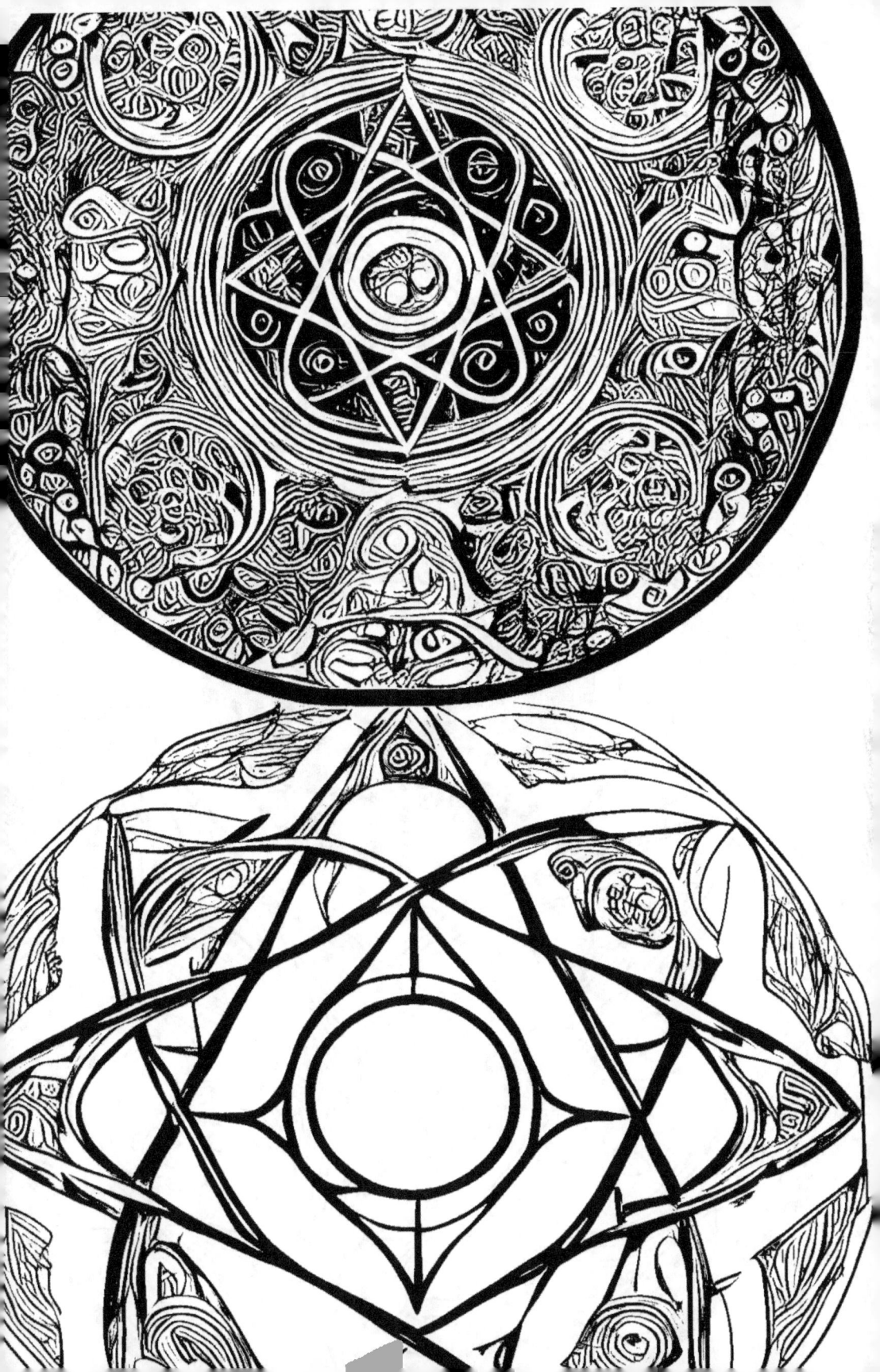

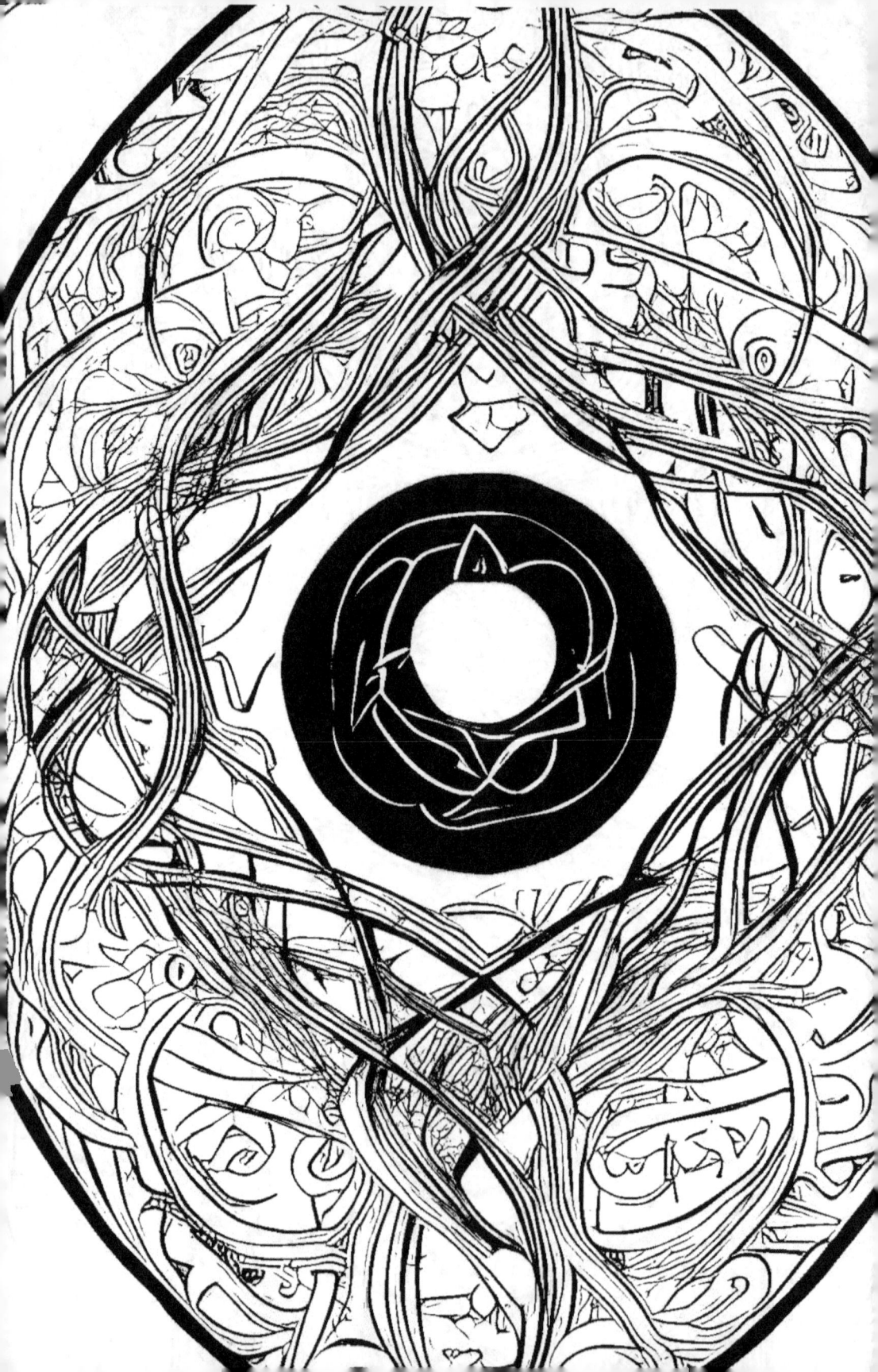

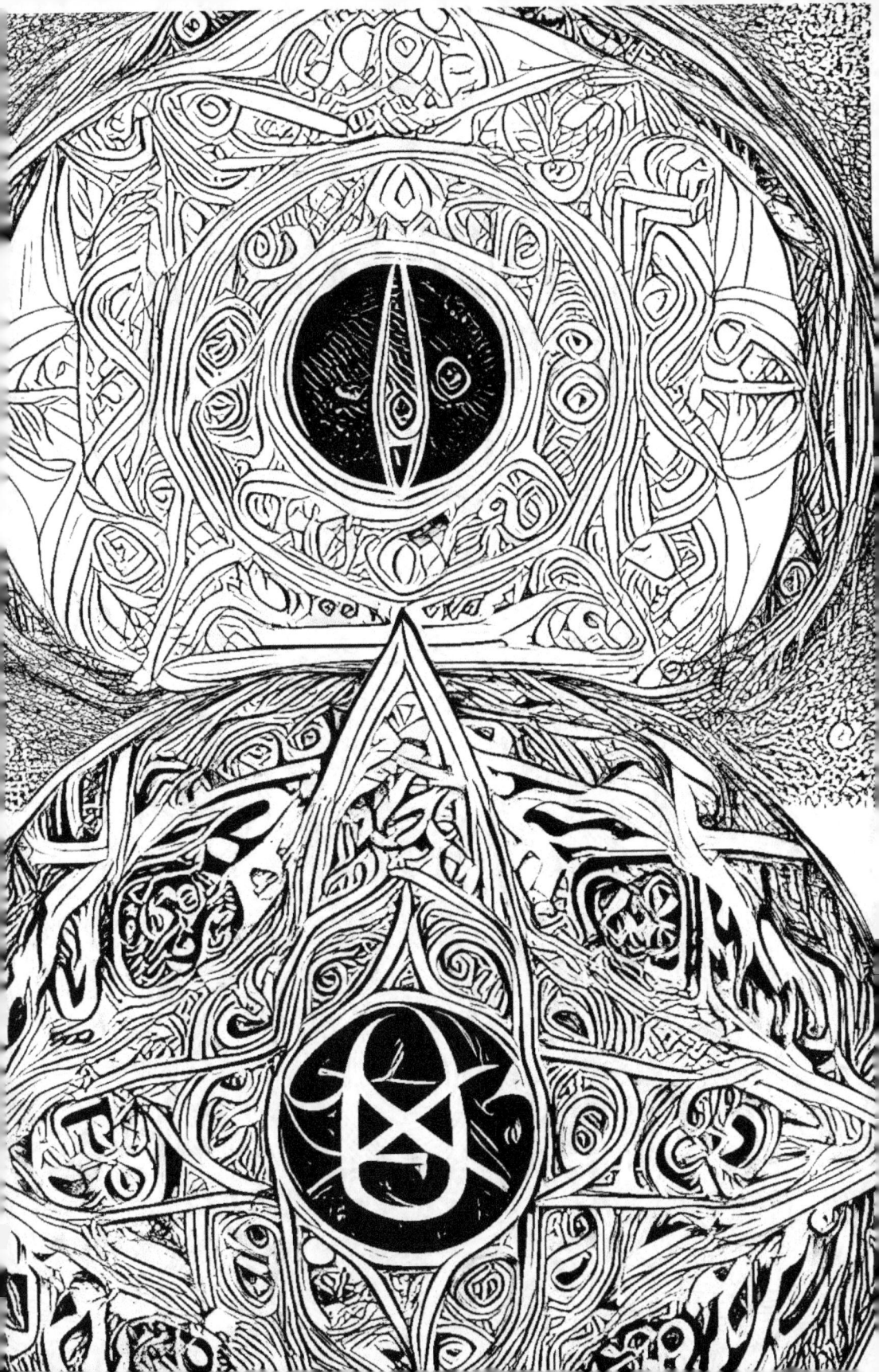

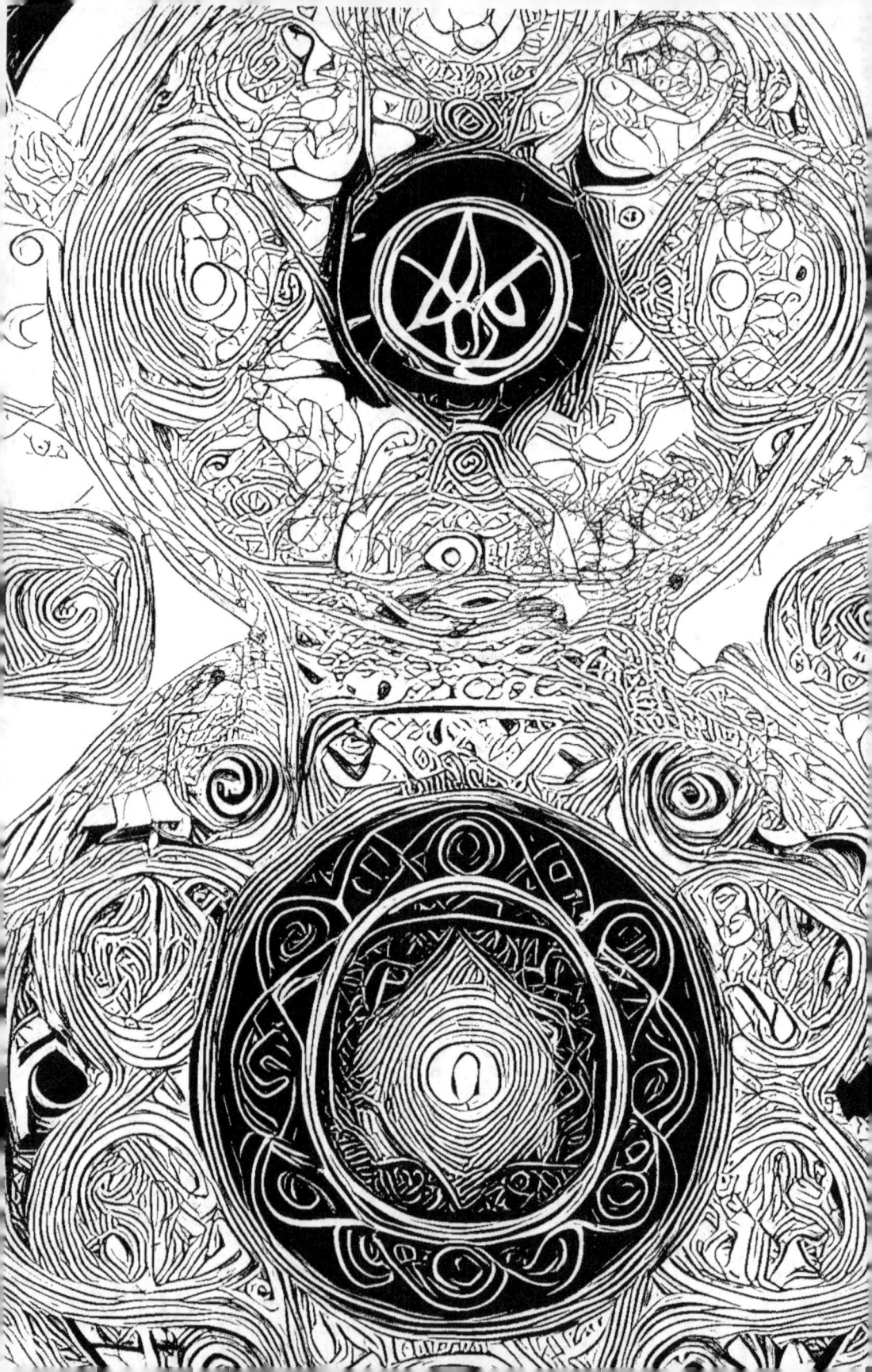

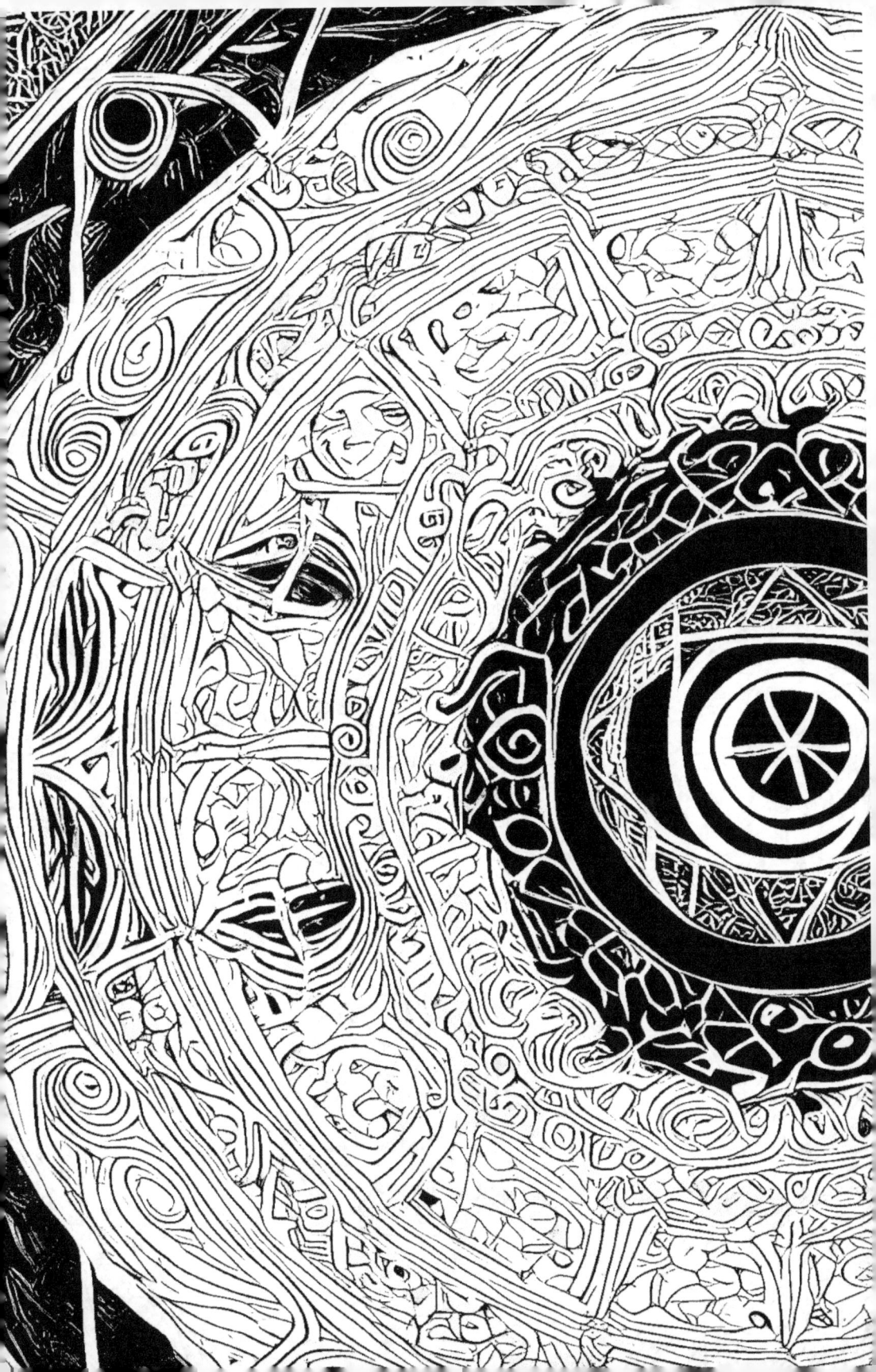

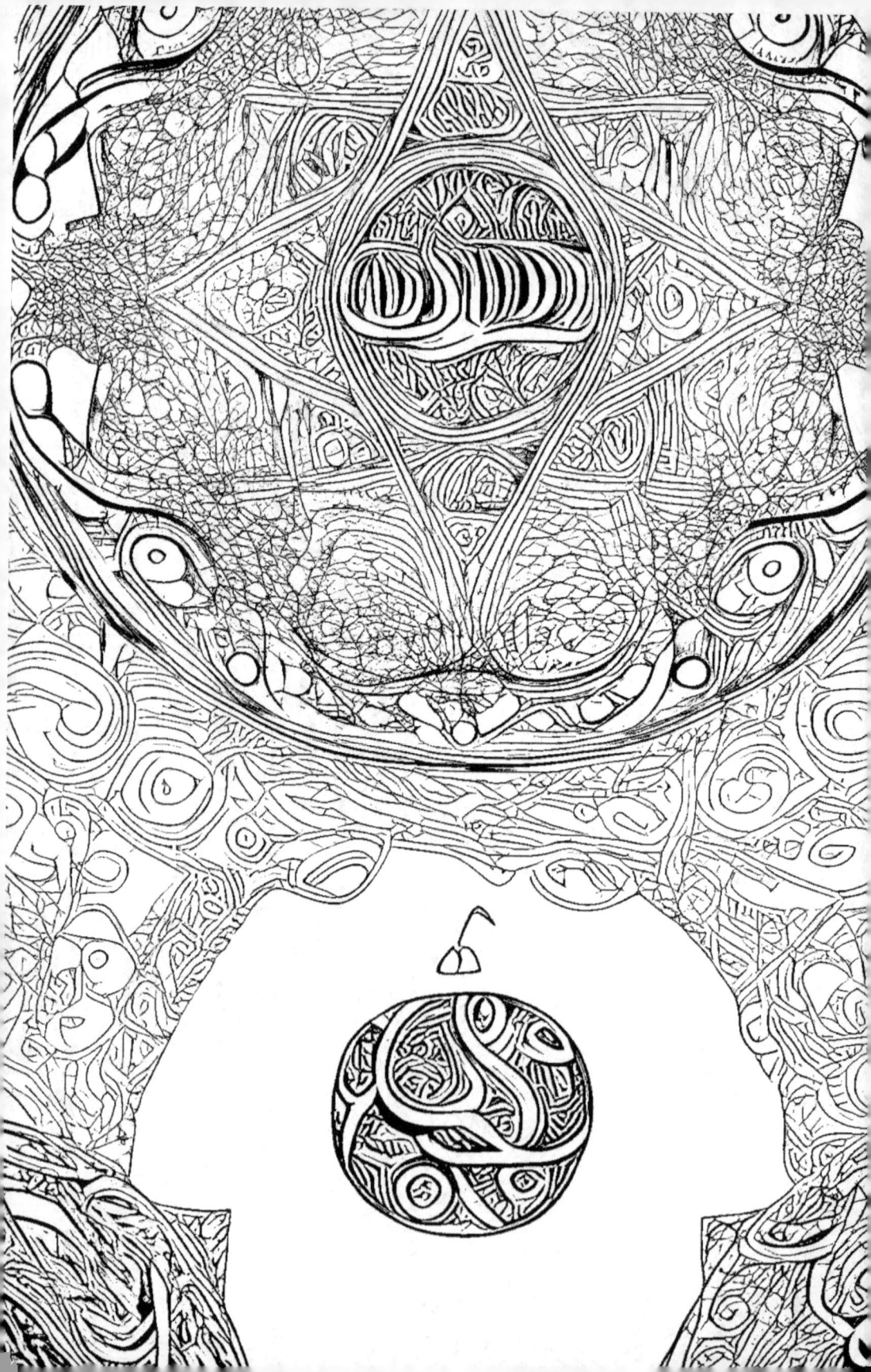

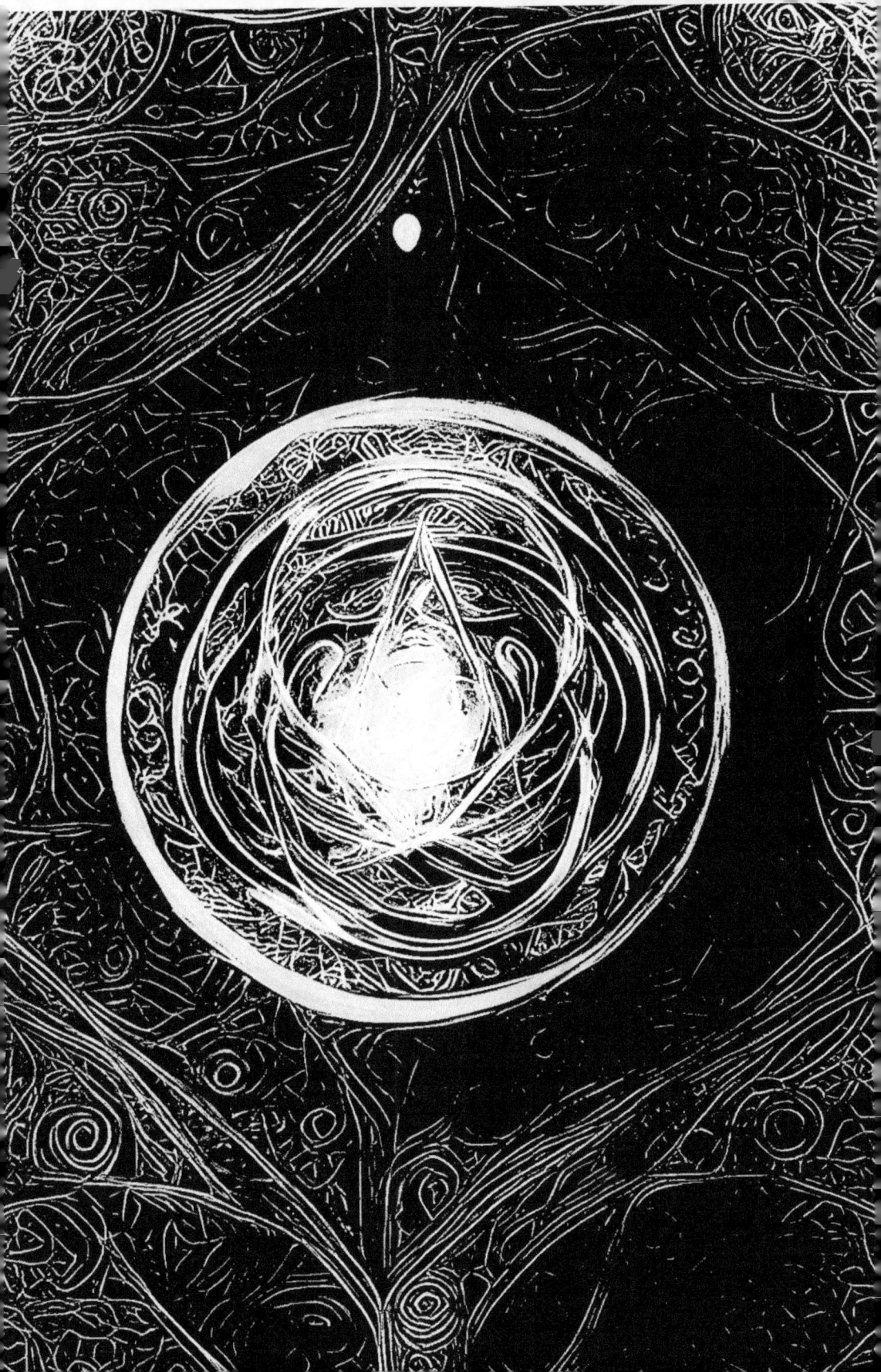

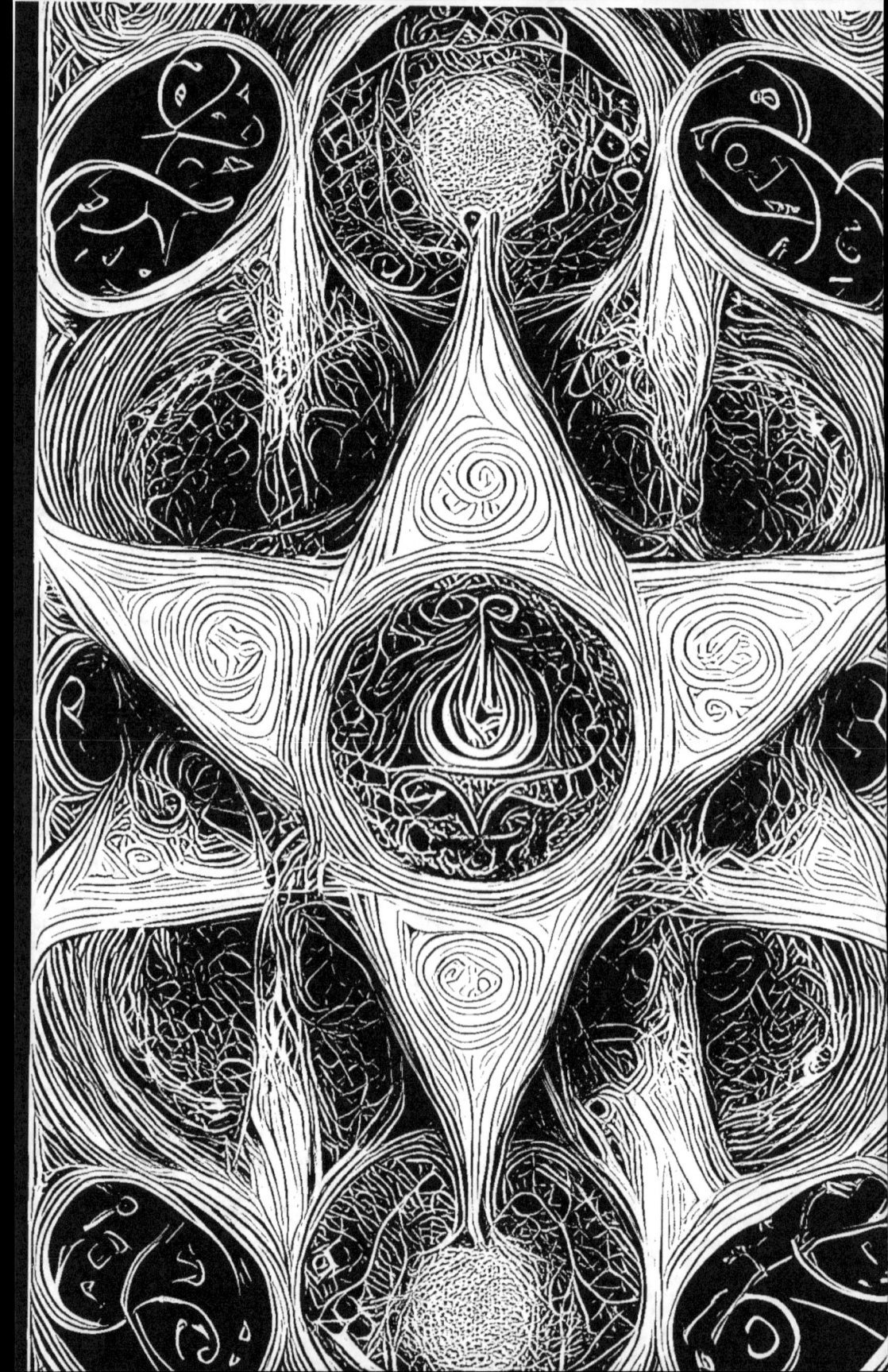

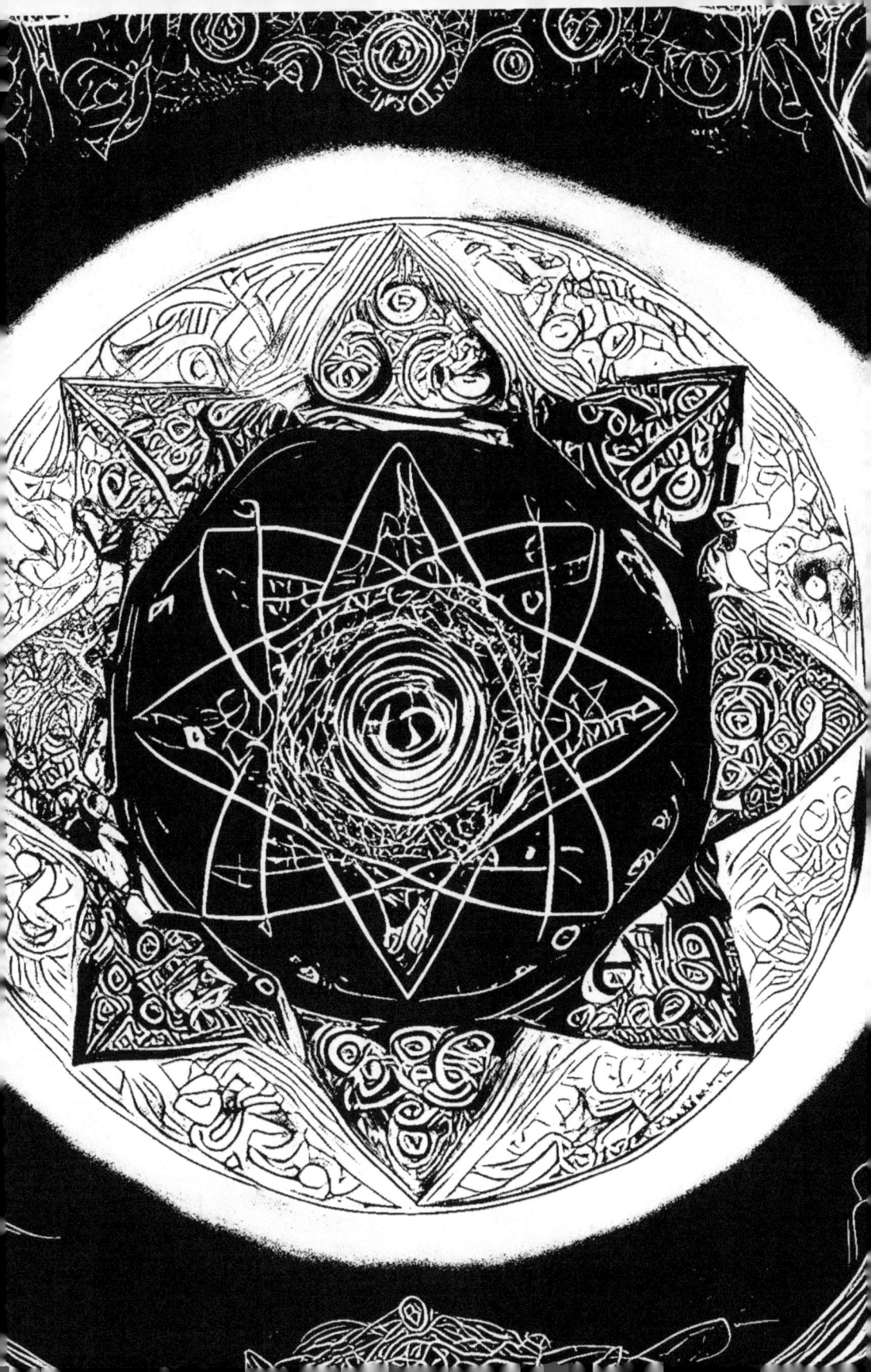

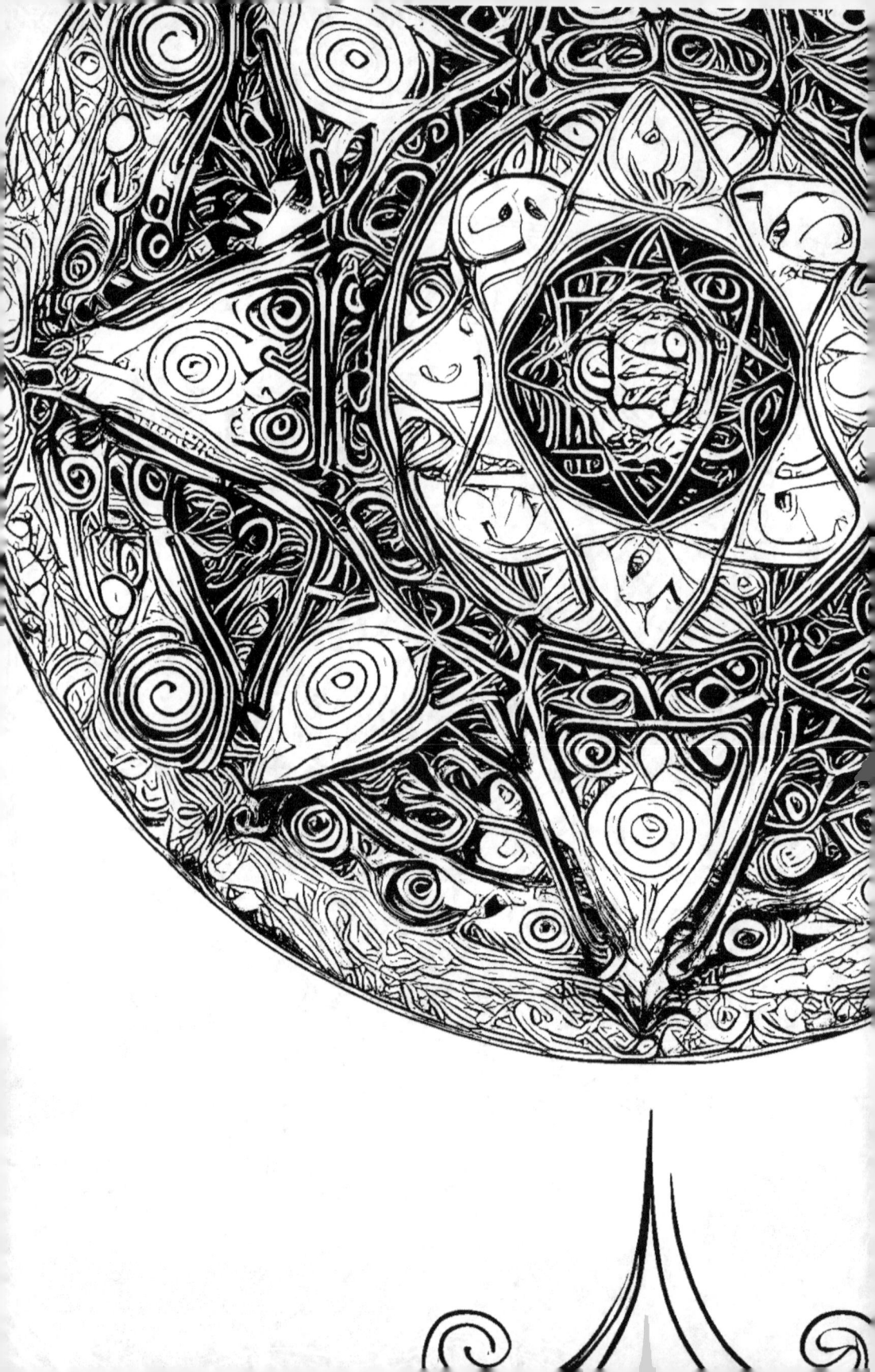

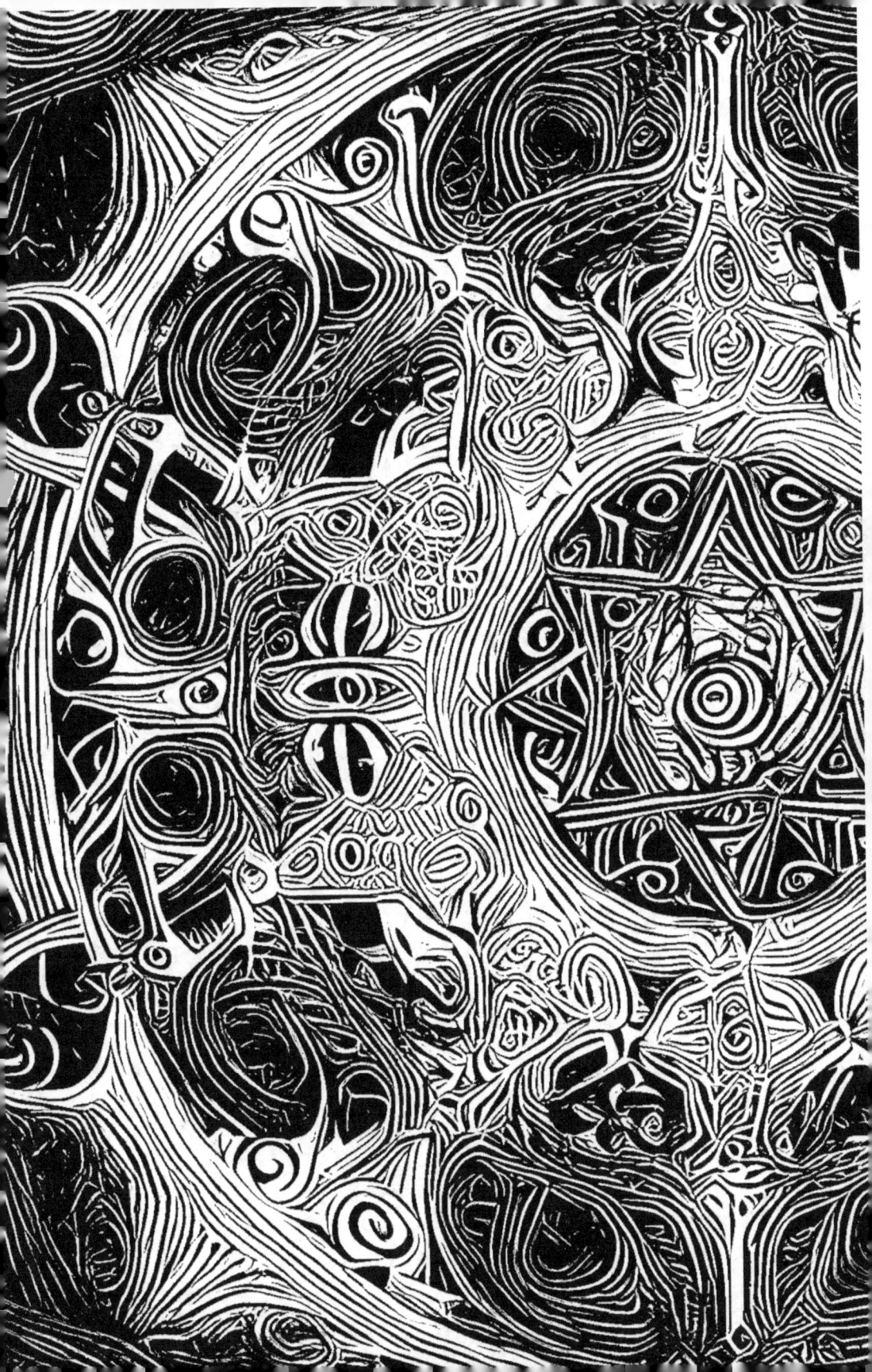

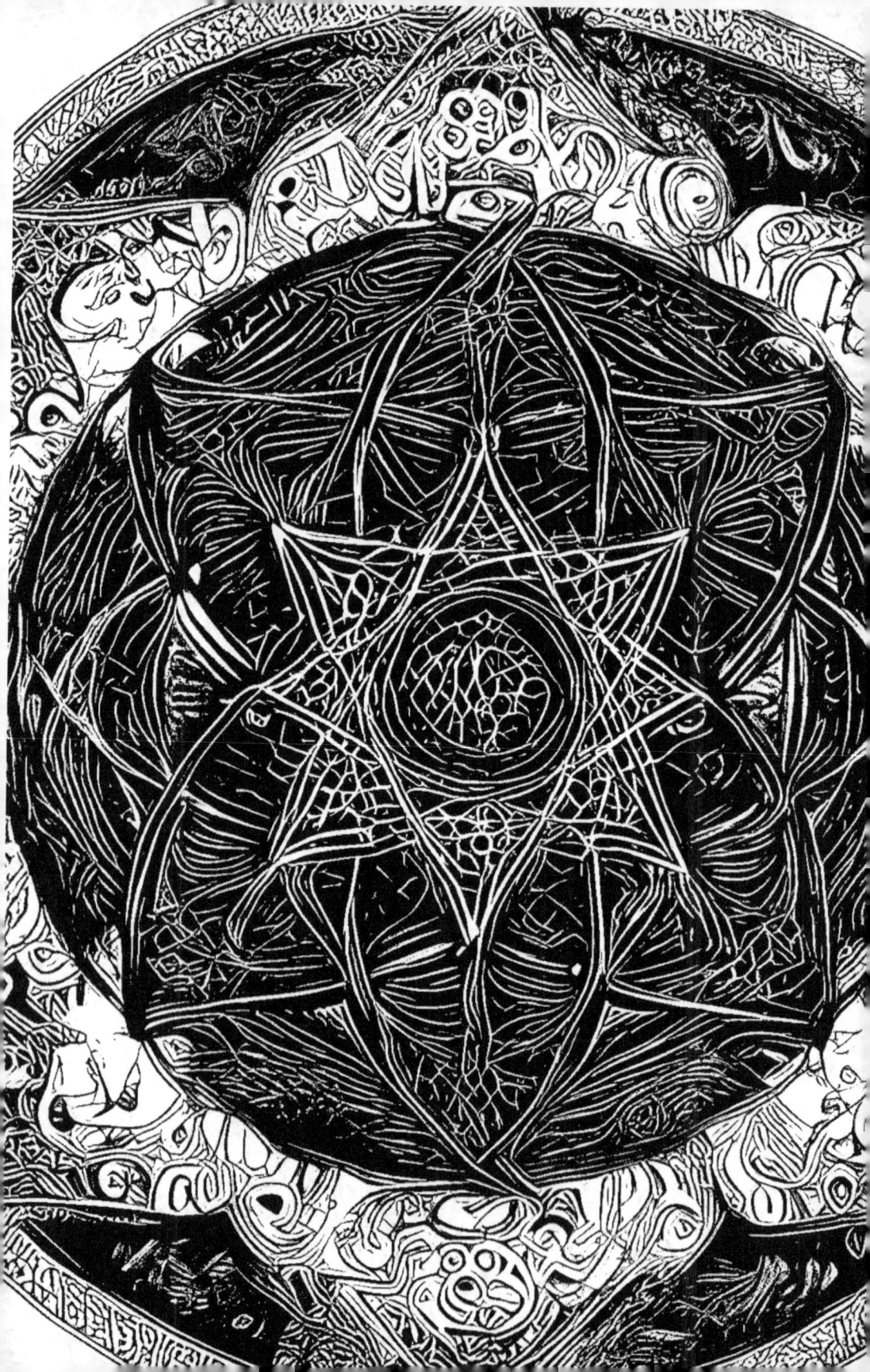

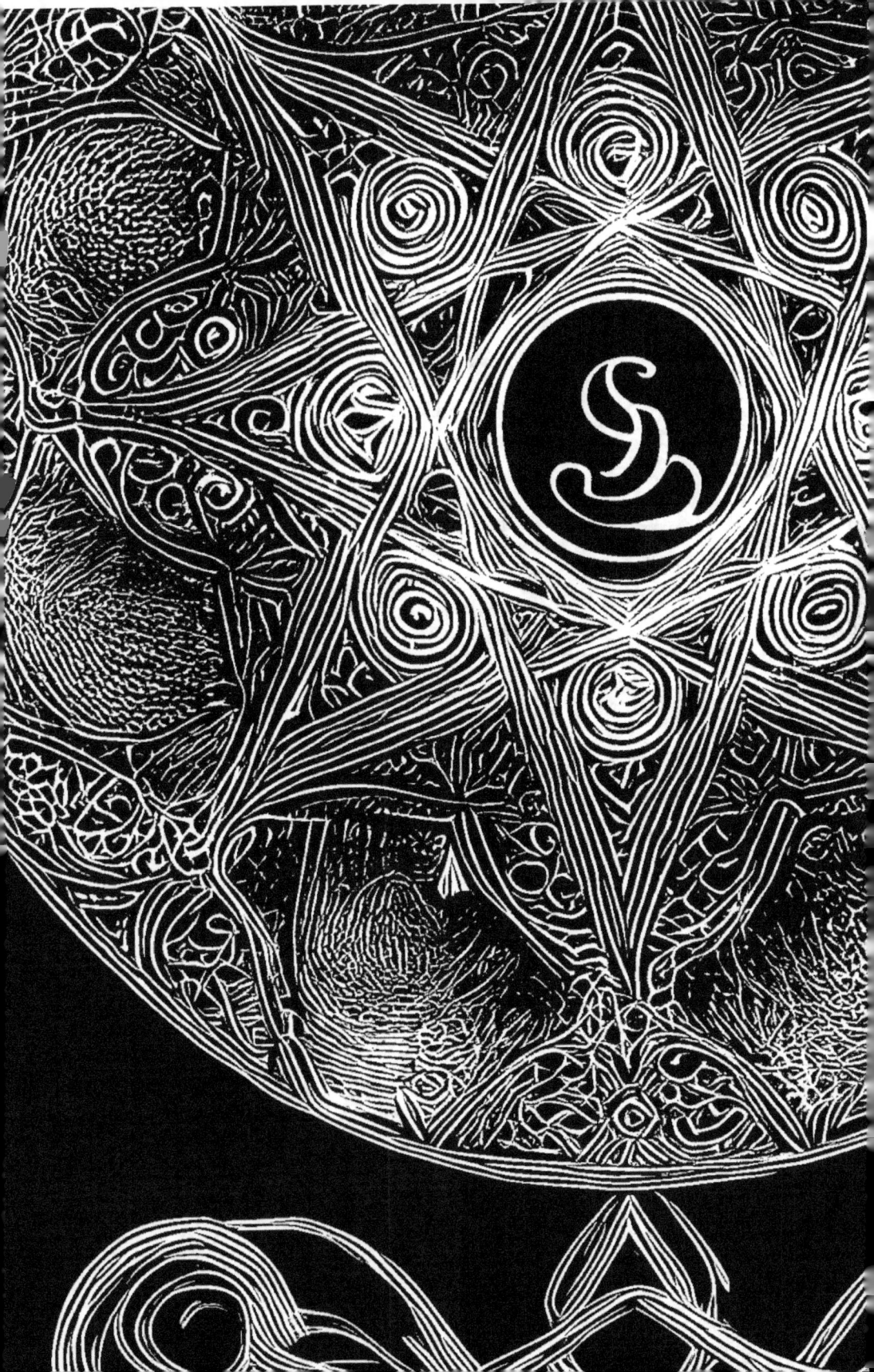

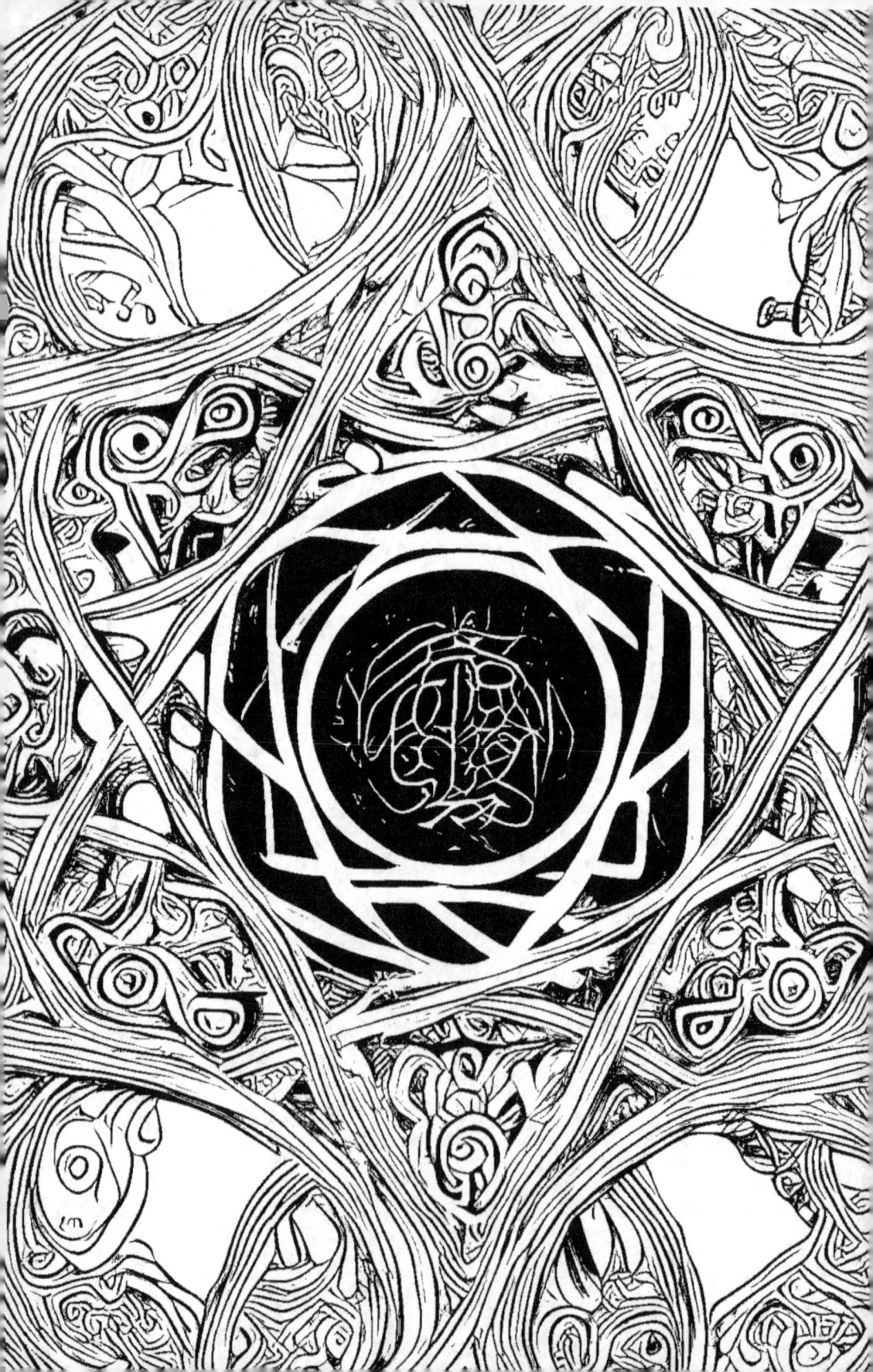

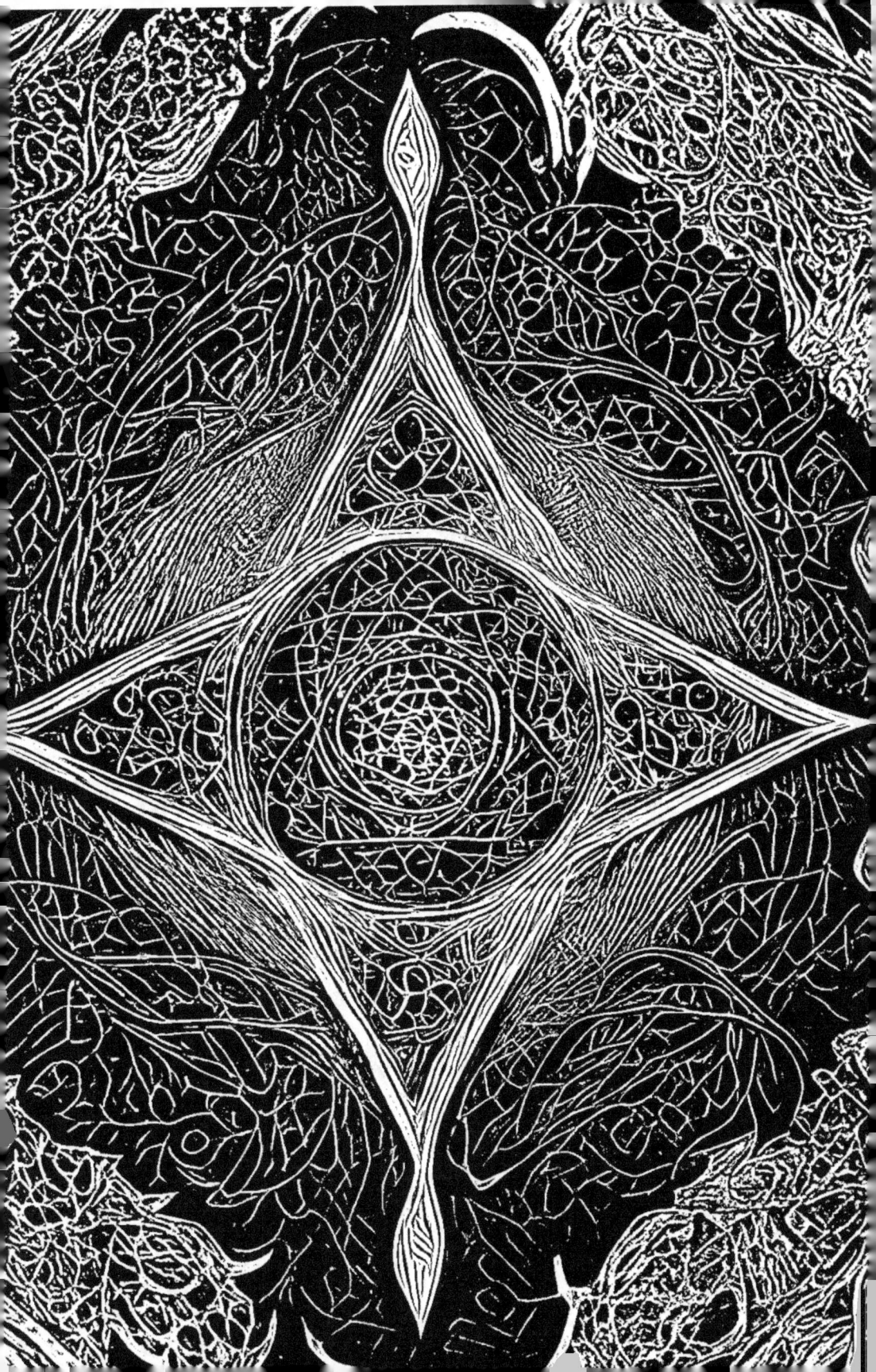

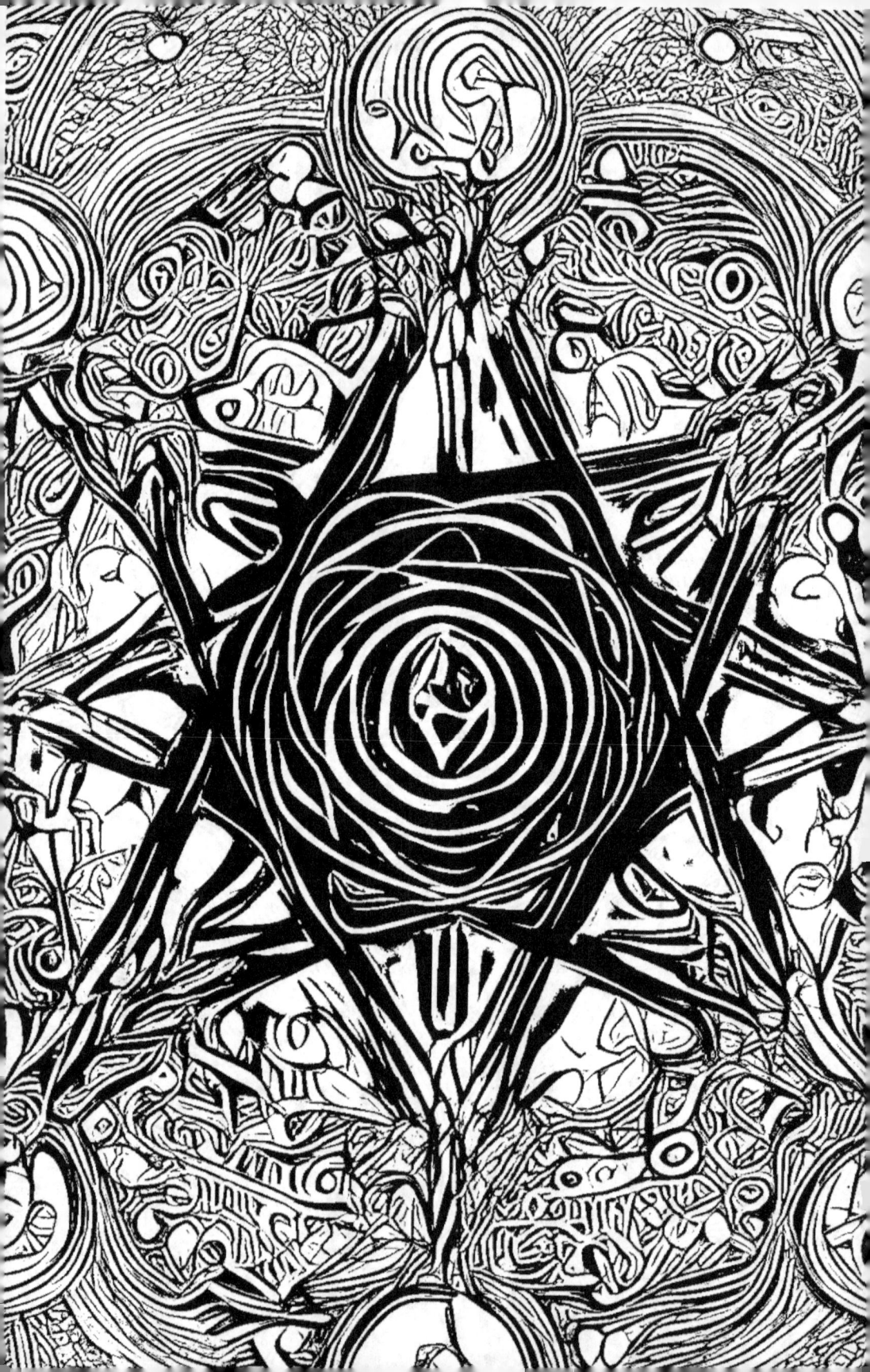

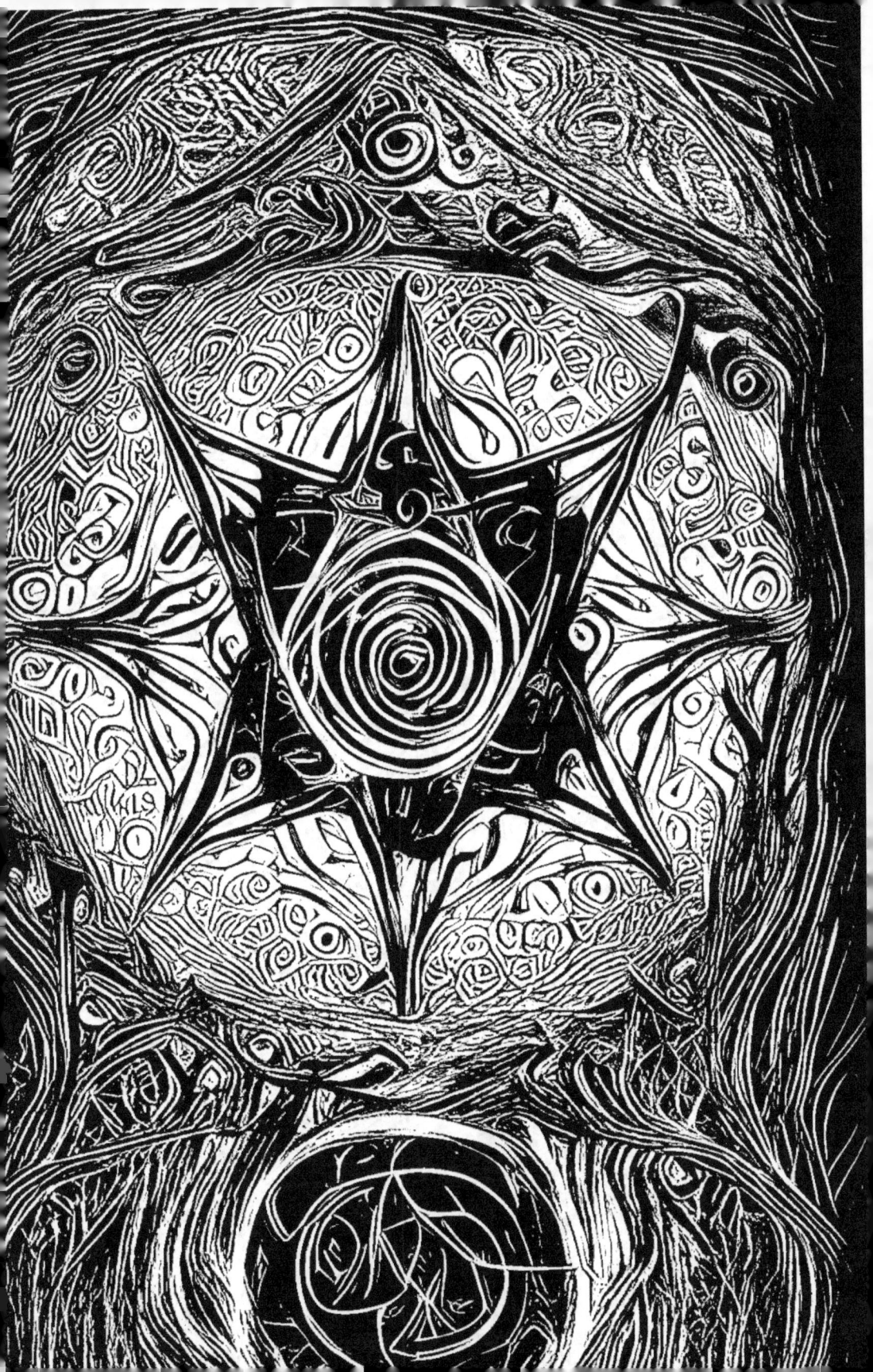

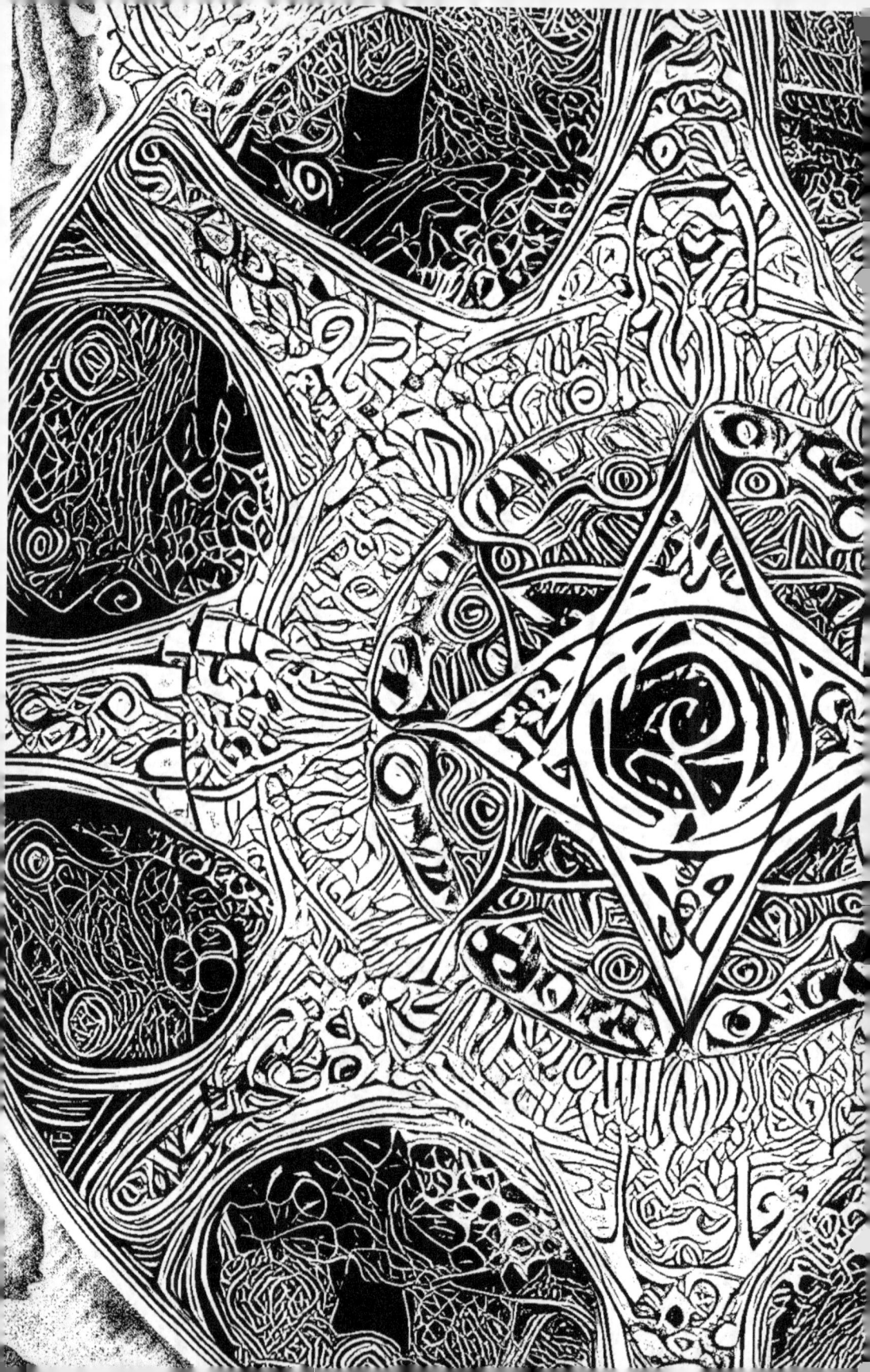

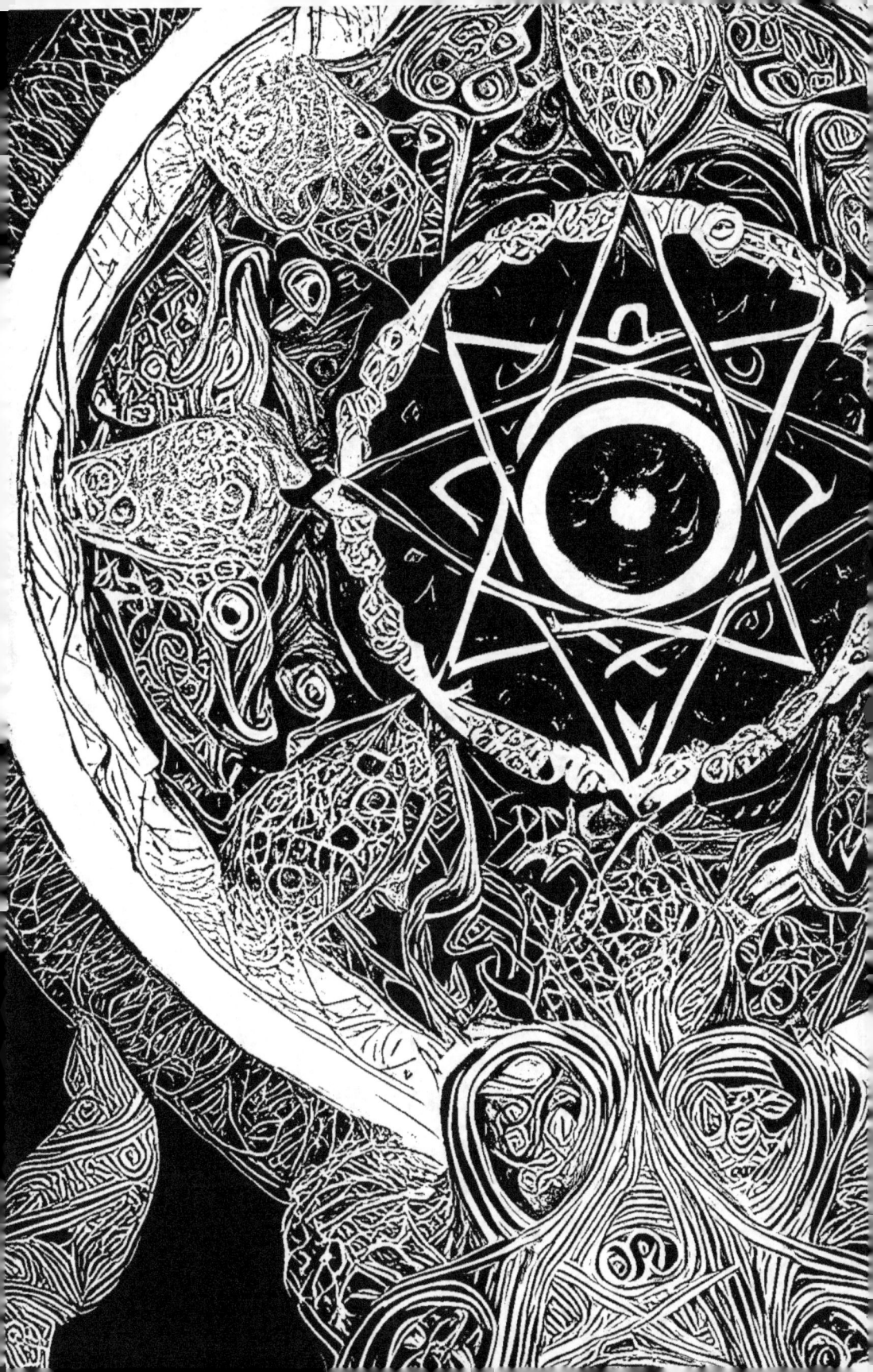

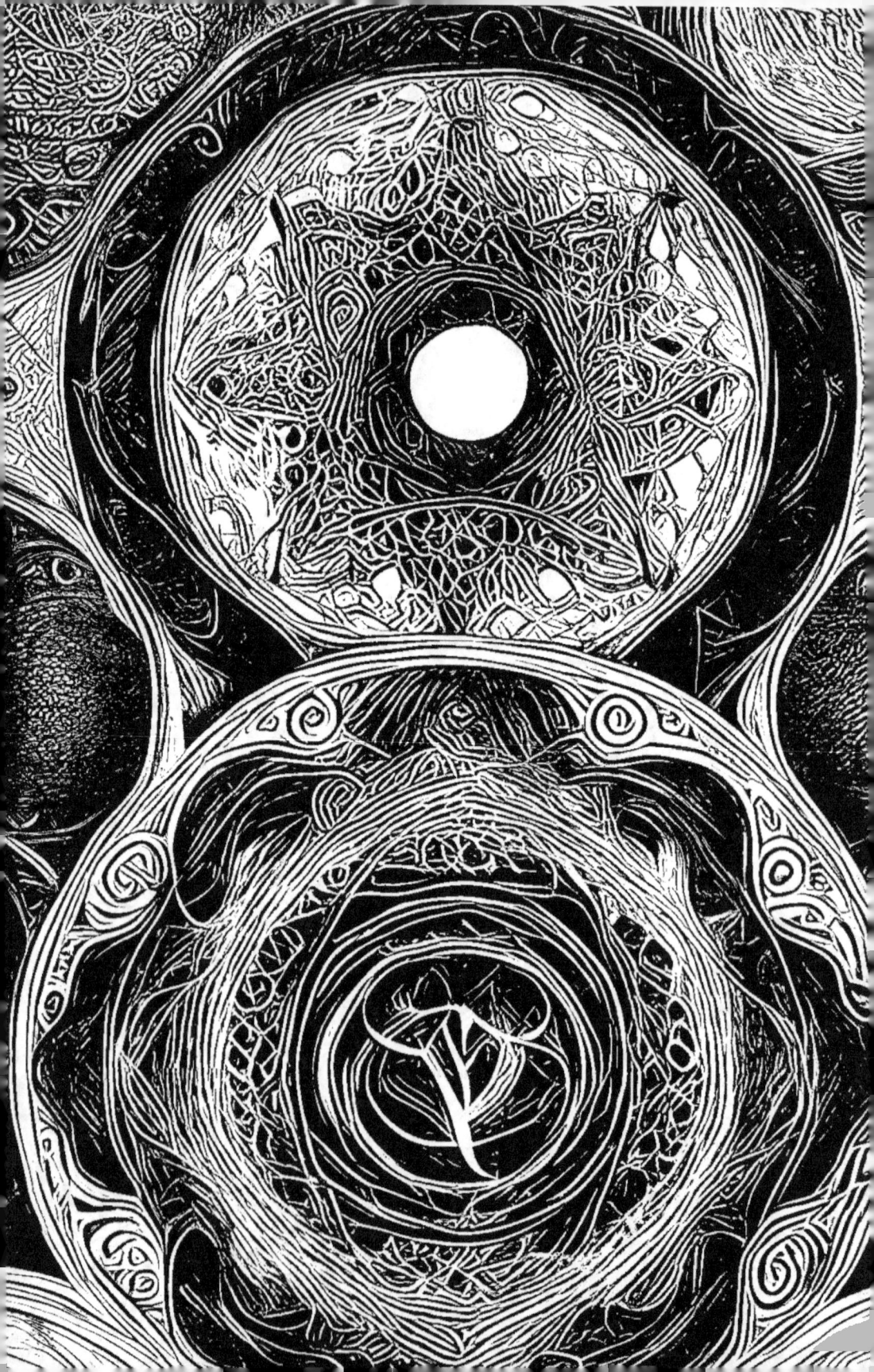

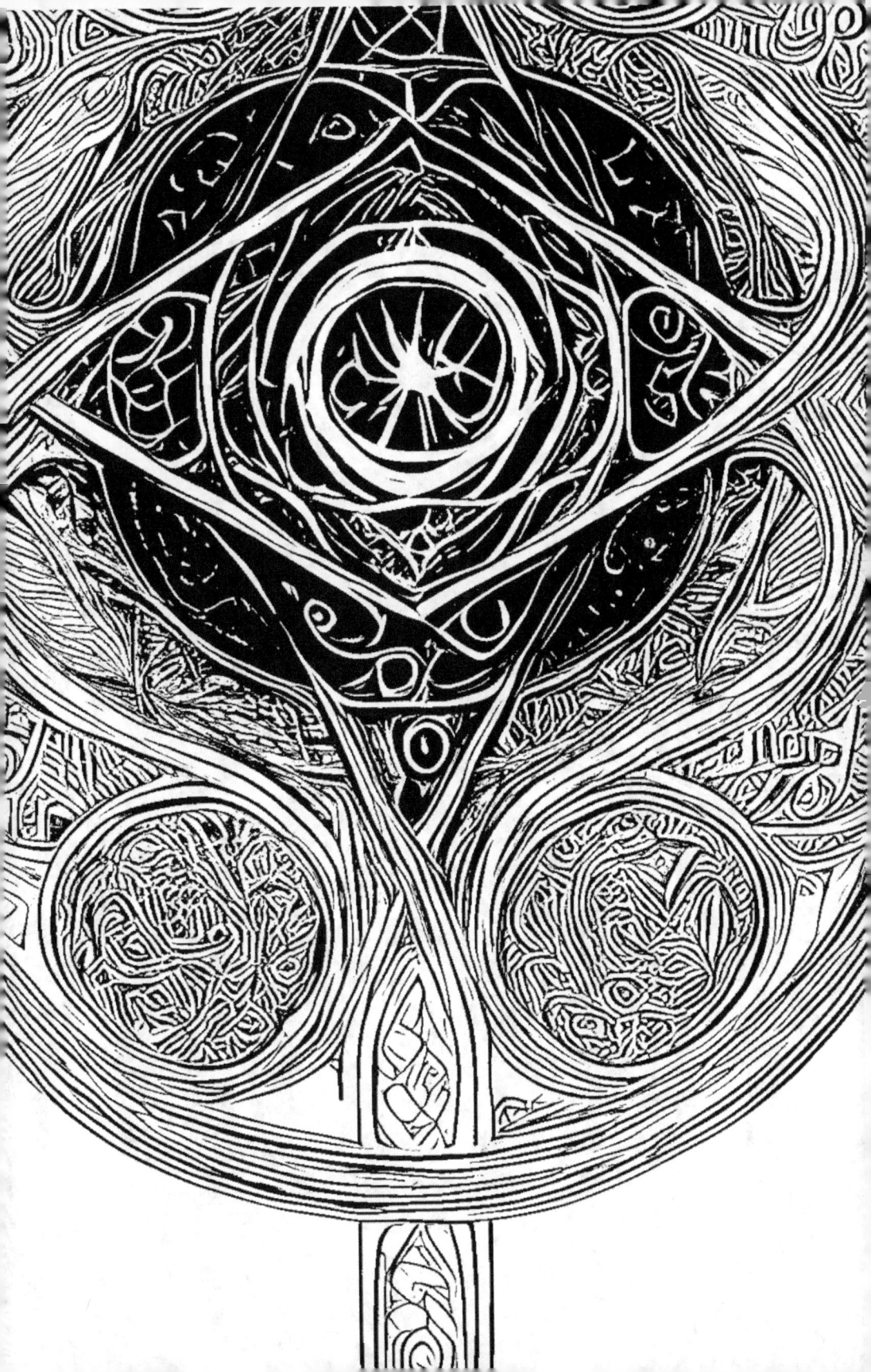

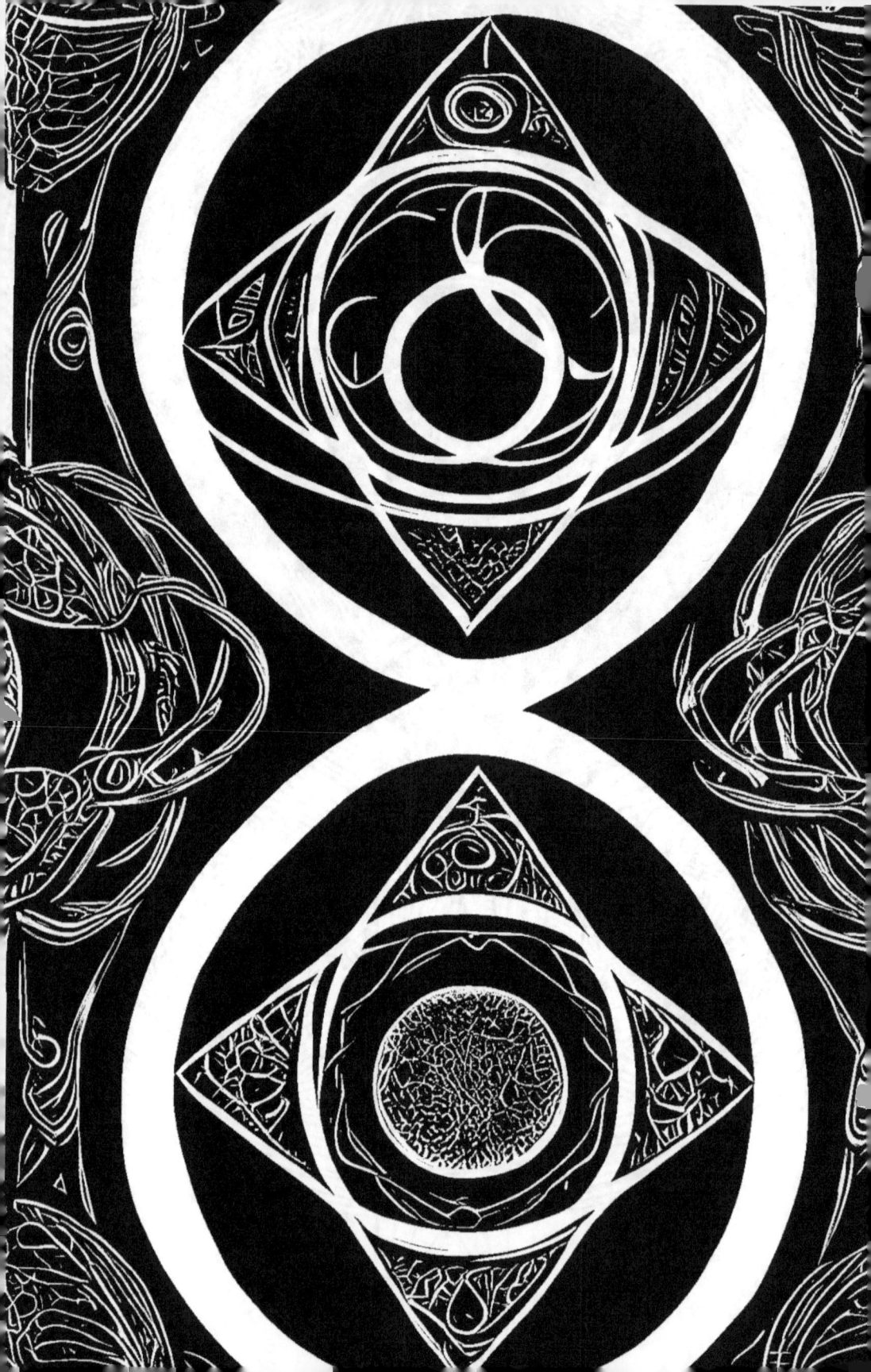

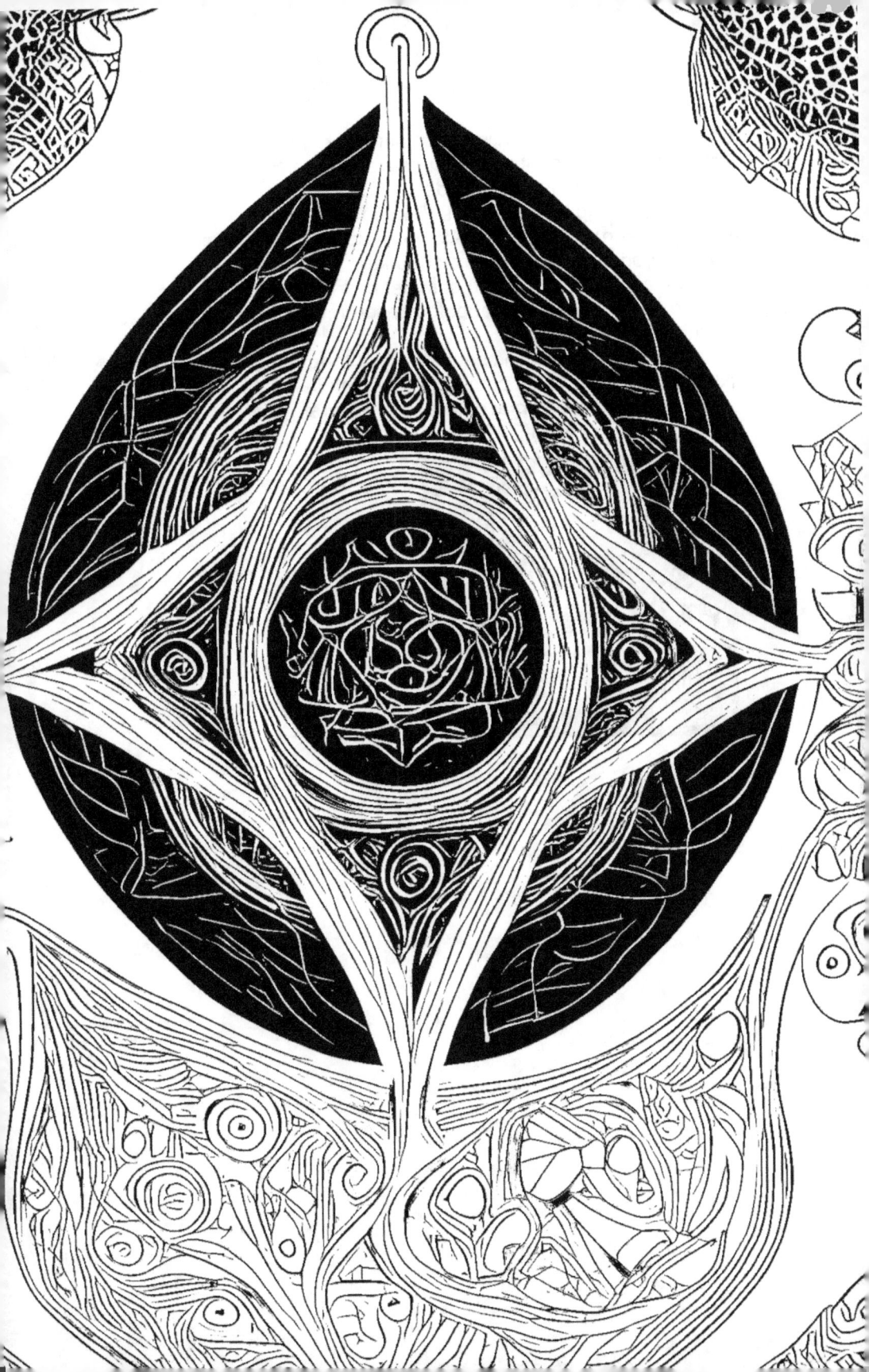

jeremyburt@ishopdailyonline.com jburt_01@hotmail.com
Make Money Online: https://ishopdailyonline.com
Print On Demand: https://ishopdaily.redbubble.com
Print On Demand @ Etsy: https://ishopdailyonline.etsy.com
dj12mind Instrumental Music Albums: https://dj12mind.com
Affiliate Products: https://index.ishopdailyonline.com
Patreon: https://www.patreon.com/user?u=80194438
Facebook: https://www.facebook.com/jeremy.burt2
Youtube:
https://www.youtube.com/channel/UCwV3nApPDh3dNHUGIX4w5nA
tiktok: https://www.tiktok.com/@jeremyburt4?lang=en
amazon: https://www.amazon.com/author/jeremyburt
THANK YOU FOR CHECKING IT OUT!

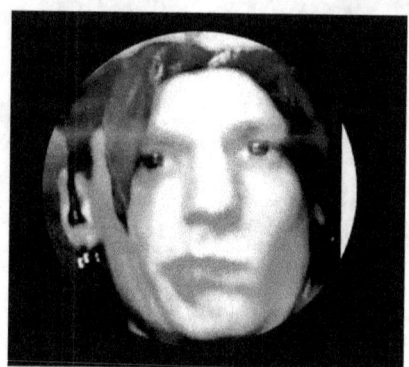